The

FACES

of

RAGE

DAVID DAMICO

NAVPRESS

A MINISTRY OF THE NAVIGATORS

P.O.BOX 35001, COLORADO SPRINGS, COLORADO 80935

© 1992 by David Damico
All rights reserved. No part of this publication may be reproduced in any form without written permission from NavPress, P.O. Box 35001, Colorado Springs, CO 80935.
Library of Congress Catalog Card Number: 91-67289
ISBN 08910-96671

FOR A FREE CATALOG OF
NAVPRESS BOOKS & BIBLE STUDIES,
CALL TOLL FREE 1-800-366-7788 (USA)
or 1-416-499-4615 (CANADA)

*"On the day you were born your cord was not cut,
nor were you washed with water to make you clean,
nor were you rubbed with salt or wrapped in cloths.
No one looked on you with pity or had compassion
enough to do any of these things for you. Rather,
you were thrown out into the open field, for on the day
you were born you were despised.
"Then I passed by and saw you kicking about in
your blood, and as you lay there in your blood
I said to you, 'Live!'. . .
"Later I passed by, and when I looked at you
and saw that you were old enough for love, I spread
the corner of my garment over you and covered your
nakedness. I gave you my solemn oath and entered
into a covenant with you, declares the Sovereign LORD,
and you became mine.
"I bathed you with water and washed
the blood from you and put ointments on you. I clothed
you with an embroidered dress and put leather sandals
on you. I dressed you in fine linen and covered you
with costly garments. . . . And your fame spread
among the nations on account of your beauty, because
the splendor I had given you made your beauty perfect,
declares the Sovereign LORD."*

Ezekiel 16:4-6,8-10,14

To Owen M.

Whose significant and sudden loss on March 27, 1991, immersed me in a pool of familiar grief whose first and most basic element—mortality—dissolves even the best woven garment of omnipotence, benign or otherwise. Naked in my own felt helplessness, I heard the two small, universal words *No* and *Why*, each punctuated with mustard seeds of resistance that can become a tree of rage.

I am indebted to Owen for his patience at my feeble attempts to comfort and my awkward efforts to respect his *No* and *Why* when they resisted my inoculations of meaning and hope. His loss, and his openness to my company in the midst of it, injected a great deal of mercy and humility into the pages you are about to read.

Contents

Foreword

GOD HAS A GREAT world in which we are each meant to be irreplaceable and play a significant role. Eternal life, the undying life of God, comes to those who release themselves into God's hands by trusting Jesus and following Him into a life of loving service within the relationships that make up their lives. Jesus taught the basic truth that we are created to live beyond ourselves: "Unless a grain of wheat falls into the earth and decomposes, nothing comes of it; but if it loses itself in the earth, it produces much fruit."

But we quickly find that when we extend ourselves to others, even in the relationships of childhood, we are easily hurt—often tragically wounded. This fills us with fear and anger and leads us to seek strategies of control. What we cannot "engulf," to use the book's useful terminology, we "abandon."

The integrity or wholeness of life that God intends us to achieve by living with Him where we can (and will) be hurt—caring for, relying on, being accessible to those around us—we then try to achieve by organizing our lives

7

around our losses and our anger. Rage becomes "father and mother, teacher and counselor, friend and companion."

And in our rage *we* take control. At least we try. We intend to manage our lives, but instead only fragment and paralyze our souls. We cannot have a life with others on condition that we control the relationships. Others usually have the same idea anyway. Yet we desperately need relationship, no matter how angry and fearful we may be. And the strength, joy, and wholeness of life will not be ours unless our relationships to others are redeemed in our relationship with God. Our strategy of control leaves us starved and weak.

David Damico's *The Faces of Rage* exposes the roots of the powerlessness that many people experience daily in relation to their own behavior. Even those with lifelong professions of faith in Christ may find their thoughts, feelings, and actions routinely taking directions where they "do what they would not and do not what they would." They feel half alive, isolated, unknown, used, helpless, guilt-ridden, ashamed, unreal.

David Damico understands that the solution cannot be just a change of behavior. Rather the deepest motivational foundations of our lives have to be revised. New currents of hope and love must begin to move in our souls. But this cannot happen until we see our defensive strategies for what they are and acknowledge that they cannot solve our problems of how to deal with loss and its wounds.

The Faces of Rage explores the deathly strategies whereby, trying to deal with loss on its own, the self closes down its access to God's provisions for redemption and health. This book opens up ways of disrupting those strategies by "crossing from grief to grace," finding abundance of life in the midst of loss and beyond.

As the illusions begin to give way, we may begin to hear clearly the good news of God's Kingdom available through reliance upon Jesus. His Kingdom accepts and absorbs our losses and our rage. We begin to put God in charge of our wholeness and integrity, begin to see fullness beyond loss, begin to *experience* it in daily life.

Thus encouraged, we find the strength to put less and less energy into defending ourselves against loss and against rage. We are prepared to let them be just what they are, as we find ourselves increasingly at home in "something bigger and more substantial than ourselves," as the author writes. We have access to our reality in the reality of the Cross where manifold loss and rage were cosmic and complete—and forever redeemed. The faces of rage are released in the face of the heavenly Father.

This book will certainly be useful to many who still organize their life around their losses and their anger. Counselors also will find many dimensions of their practices illumined by it. It is a step toward that cooperation between counseling and Christian ministry that can point the way to the healing of our existence from the greatest loss, the loss of God.

We recognize the dynamics here explored and described so incisively by David from many years of clinical practice, and attest to the psychological and scriptural soundness of what he has to say about them. Page after page stand out with particular relevance to individual clients and acquaintances, and we are excited at the prospect of making it available to them in their own journeys of the heart into wholeness. With numerous clients we have already found ourselves referring to new concepts from David's discussions, and utilizing familiar concepts in new applications. Jane works with a "survivors" group that has a store of special theories and ideas invoked over and over through the years because of their value and predictability in the growth process. David's concepts in *The Faces of Rage* will be included in the "collection." Thank you, David, from all of us.

JANE AND DALLAS WILLARD

Acknowledgments

LAST WEEK I LISTENED to prospective Supreme Court Justice Clarence Thomas give his opening speech to the U.S. Senate Confirmation Committee. I was moved to tears as I listened to him simply, clearly, and meekly read his own acknowledgments to the individuals on the timeline of his life and before his conception who made it possible for him to be in that distinguished and historically significant place. His plain and ordinary language (I didn't have to look up a single word he used) touched me at the core of my being—drawing from a well deep inside buckets that overflowed with my own profound sense of appreciation for those who have invested themselves in me. If it were not for all of them, I would not BE today.

To my mother, Marilou, and adoptive father, Lt. Col. Robert Damico, I owe my greatest debt. Having waded through the disappointments and pains of loss associated with our family's journey, I am at this venture thankful for both of you, as well as for the things you taught me. Dad, every time you hug me so hard it hurts, grab my face, kiss my cheek, and tell me you love me, I feel wanted, loved, liked, and whole. You give dignity and strength to the needy parts of my soul.

To my brother, Danny, and sister, Gina—you both mean a great deal to me. I feel your love and support.

I can't tell you what it means to me to sit here and look upon the faces of so many people who have contributed to my emotional and spiritual growth. Let me mention those who, in connection with this book, have helped keep me anchored to sanity and reality while completing such a HUGE task:

Wes Roberts of Life Enrichment in Denver, Colorado, opened a door for me that seemed otherwise impossible. Upon giving him a thumbnail overview of my "concept," he promised to present the idea to NavPress. That promise was genuine. Without his willingness to go out of his way, this unknown author would still be thinking about writing a book.

I'd like to thank NavPress. What an impressive and dedicated organization. Not only did they take a chance with me, but they gave me their best editor! (I'm allowed to be partial.) Traci Mullins had the tough task of corralling my idealism and keeping my concepts simple, concise, and understandable. To the extent that you walk away with an "Ah-hah"—you can thank Traci. If you walk away scratching your head with "What did he mean?"— that's probably me.

I always wondered why authors thanked their editors. I used to conclude that it was the "proper" thing to do. The truth is, without them, the books we all read would leave us feeling like we did after reading the philosophers whose names we couldn't pronounce in college. I always thought I was just too simple to understand the "profound" wisdom they contained. Now I know they just didn't have editors. Those poor guys were probably just as lost and confused as I was. (That is, by the way, why their hair was always so messy on the inside leaflet photograph under the caption "About the Author.")

Traci, you are priceless. I am particularly thankful to have worked with someone whose life is committed to and intimately acquainted with the concepts presented in this book. I owe its practicality and graspability to your insight and work.

For those who support me, my ministry and the vision of Christian Assisted Recovery Environments by participating in our program, I wish to offer my heartfelt thanks. To the members of my planning committee: Jo-Helen, Aubrey, Barbara, Michael, Patrice, and Kellie, for the endless hours of dedication, sacrifice, patience, encouragement, and FRIENDSHIP . . . how does one say thank you?

To the Longmire family—words cannot express the love I feel for you. I treasure the memories we have built together. Your support of me throughout the months of writing strengthened and encouraged me to finish.

Finally, my wife, Kellie—partner, friend, confidante, lover—thank you for giving me your support while I slipped, slid, and bounced through my own resolution process. You make me feel special, chosen, significant, and appreciated. I love your laugh, your smile, and your wise heart—I feel alive in your presence. I am forever and always yours.

Introduction

WHAT DO YOU THINK of when you hear the word *rage*? Most of us picture rage as being out of control. Almost all of us can remember feeling rage at one time or another. It's the sudden explosion of emotion we experience when someone cuts us off on the freeway or treats us rudely in public. It's the last straw our children seem to find at five o'clock every afternoon. It's the tolerance limit business clients push with the last-minute request, "Can you do me a quick favor?"—meaning, "Where do you think you're going? I'm not done taking advantage of you." It's the rising volcanic material that threatens to spew forth its destructive expletives to blast anyone in close proximity.

But rage is so much more.

Many myths surrounding rage make a book like this one difficult to write. Perhaps the biggest myths are that rage is always a red-eyed, fire-breathing dragon; it belongs to neurotics and bullies who can't control themselves; and "normal" Christians don't have a relationship with it.

Having examined my own misconceptions about rage, I have had to adjust or reconstruct much of my thinking. The idea that rage could ever have a friendly face or be a source of comfort did not fit my view of things until I recognized the many roles rage played in my own life. I discovered that rage not only could be docile and peace-loving, but also could function as a benevolent personal protector. If I felt threatened or afraid, rage gave me advice or struck out against the danger. Never mind that the protection I felt rage offered me was a false and fragile one. Rage can be both warrior and peacemaker. It can be the proverbial wolf in sheep's clothing.

I would have passed by a book like this one several years ago, thinking, *I'm sure glad I'm a Christian. This is one book I don't need to read. After all, I finally have things under control.* At that time, I hadn't had a rageful outburst in some time. My red-headed, volcanic temper seemed to be dormant. However, that was before I discovered that rage is not just about angry emotion—it is about self-protection, which has more of my devotion than I like to admit. Rage blooms in the deep soil of unresolved loss—something I also had a lot more of than I realized.

In my struggle to protect myself against the hostile world, I realized that I turned to a parent other than God for safety. I eventually discovered that parent to be rage—not always the fire-breathing, flame-throwing kind (that was easy enough to see), but the more benevolent protector displaying faces appropriate to the threat or danger at any given moment. The discovery that most of my daily interactions as an evangelical Christian for twenty years were rage-driven was a real blow to my spirituality.

While I could identify and ruefully recount past events when I struck out at other human beings in white-hot rage, I could barely see the more subtle and "acceptable" defense mechanisms that were part of the same beast. I was stunned and humiliated to discover that in nearly every arena of my life and relationships, I functioned in a self-protecting, self-preserving mode, often totally unconcerned about powerfully and righteously loving others. This discovery also left me with a chilling question: If rage has been my parent, tutor, confidant, counselor, and defender, where is God and what has His role been?

Over the past few years, I have spent thousands of hours in groups with men and women who wrestle with questions and conflicts much like my own, and I have discovered we all have something in common besides our faith—a thriving inner rage. We didn't all have the courage or insight to call it that. For many of us, *rage* was a stigmatizing, shameful word. Even if we identified ourselves as rageful, we were reluctant to admit what we did in those rageful moments. We learned to frame the word in softer tones in hopes that it would go away, sometimes vowing to prevent its future interference with our otherwise normal lives.

If we were prone to explosion, we viewed our rageful outbursts (when reason returned) as foreign. We nervously queried, "Where did that come from?" and assured survivors that such demonic behavior was not our standard operating procedure. We vowed restraint and worked diligently to maintain control. We looked for ways to defang, declaw, and chain the inner lion. Unfortunately, we tended to view success as superficially conquering rage. If the lion roared, let him roar in anonymity; by all means don't let anyone see what might be interpreted as a vestige of the old rageful self.

One thing I have learned in my work with people courageous enough to reveal their inner selves is this: *Rage is as ordinary as the common cold and neither vows of self-control nor confessing the name of Jesus in militaristic determination will effect a lasting cure.* Rage must be pulled out by its roots—and its roots are buried deep in the painful territory of unresolved loss that most of us don't care to visit.

Not everyone will find this book digestible. Some will hold to the appearance of rage as the harmless "sheep" and never see the ravenous "wolf" that waits to gain the trust of its next unsuspecting victim. I have written in hopes that the insights and observations provided will forewarn and prepare you, not only to recognize and eradicate the many faces of rage you encounter in yourself and in others, but more importantly to help you experience the authentic, unsullied presence of Jesus Christ in your relationships. This is measurable, in my view, if the result of your reading brings about Christlike love and fellowship.

I have devoted my life and work to this task: to equip the Body of Christ to do the work of loving within the context of truthful and supportive community. Since I am a disciple in the making, I have much to learn about such things and hope that you will sense me walking alongside you as we unmask the faces of rage. After all, this is a family affair.

PART ONE

▼

LOSS:
Why Are We Rageful?

CHAPTER 1
The Nature of Loss

CHAPTER 2
Eight Significant Losses

CHAPTER 3
Five Ways We Experience Loss

CHAPTER 4
How Unresolved Loss
Visits the Next Generation

▼

The Nature of Loss

BRETT'S PARENTS DIVORCED when he was seven. Brett's dad left the state, and his mom went to work, leaving him all alone after school every day. When she came home, she was tired, irritable, and depressed. She would say, "Brett, why don't you call the pizza place and order what you want for dinner tonight. I just don't feel like cooking." Brett got cards from his dad on his birthday, but did not speak to him on the telephone. His dad called about once a week, but always got in a fight with his mother on the phone. She would cry, hang up on him, and say something like, "Don't ever trust men for anything. They'll hurt you every time."

▼

Mike was getting beat up at school every day by a bully three grades older. An only child, he was small for his age. Each time Mike came home from school, his mother would clean him up and tell him he shouldn't fight. When Mike would try to explain that he didn't start it, she would reply it didn't matter. He must have been doing something to egg on the bully and should just mind his own business.

Mike's father would give him a different message: "You are going to have to learn to fight your own battles. Maybe if you get beat up enough, you'll get the courage to fight back." After Mike came home for a week with torn clothing and an occasional bloody nose or lip, his dad took him out to the garage and scolded him for being such a sissy. He told Mike that if he came home again looking like that, he would be spanked. He left the garage saying, "No son of mine is going to be a sissy," and closed the door behind him on a confused and helpless young boy.

——▼——

Both of Jane's parents worked. They left the house early in the morning and returned late at night. Jane was the oldest of three children. She was responsible for getting them off to school, cleaning house, fixing meals, doing laundry, and shopping. She remembered being in charge as early as age eight, when her twin brothers were born. Because the family was poor, everyone had to do his or her fair share. Jane didn't complain because she learned early that life was hard and there were no free tickets.

Jane's parents were both kind people. They seemed sorry that life was so difficult, but it did not change the facts. Jane left home as soon as her brothers were old enough to help support the family.

——▼——

George wet his bed until he was sixteen years old. It was almost a nightly occurrence for as long as he could remember. He hadn't thought for some years about the humiliation and shame he suffered for most of his childhood. He'd almost forgotten about it until his six-year-old son, Eric, began wetting his bed. George didn't know what to do. He wanted to make him stop, but he knew how hard it was as he remembered all of the shameful things his parents tried to get him to stop. Nothing worked.

George couldn't talk to Eric about the problem, although it cried out for attention. He especially couldn't tell Eric that he'd had the same problem; he hadn't told anyone, not even his wife. He simply ignored it and hoped it would go away. However, in order to ignore the bed wetting, he had to ignore Eric. He had a difficult time separating the two. Eventually he found it difficult to talk to Eric, look at him, or include him in any of his plans.

NO ESCAPE FROM LOSS

These four stories have one important thing in common—they're all illustrations of loss. Life has been different for each of us. How would you summarize your life in a paragraph or two? What would you highlight as tragic, significant, ordinary, or unforgettable? For some, the pictures are clear, bright, and full of "happy times." For others, they are dull, torn, confusing, and full of strife and pain. Still others have none. The pages are blank—the pictures lost somewhere in a mental archive whose location has been carefully forgotten.

Scan the brief histories of Brett, Mike, Jane, and George. What do you see? Divorce, abandonment, single parents struggling to make ends meet, depression, isolation, legal irresponsibility, illness, death, bed-wetting, abuse in public school, poverty, and children who are raising other children. These issues make headlines every day. They touch all of us. If they haven't directly touched us, they have touched someone we know intimately. If we live in this world there is one thing we cannot escape—loss.

You might be thinking, is this going to be another one of those books that tells us how messed up things are? I hope not. It is designed to do more than just paint a picture of the problem. Reading about loss may not be fun, but it is necessary because the inability or refusal to face and resolve loss sets the stage for rage.

Sooner or later, we all lose something of value to us. Our culture ignores loss until it happens. When it does, we seem surprised, as though we were convinced, "Maybe I'll be one of the lucky ones." I believe this reflects a hidden dread. We view loss of any kind as bad and somehow believe that people who lose must be bad. This is even reflected in our language. When something tragic happens, we say, "Wasn't that a shame—she was such a young girl, too. Seemed to have everything going for her. Getting involved with that wild young man was really a bad decision. She might be here to graduate with her classmates had it not been for that."

When loss occurs, especially unexpected and tragic loss, we try to put the wild animal of loss back in a cage, at a safe distance from us and those we love. Somehow, if we can ignore it or explain it, we don't have to be so affected by it.

More than how we deal with loss, this book addresses how we *don't* deal with it. We'll talk about the manner in which loss, when left unresolved, sets the stage for patterns of avoidance that keep loss and the emotion connected with it at arm's length, enabling us to recolor our world to eliminate any trace of loss having visited us. This emotional resistance to loss sets up a mechanism of avoidance called *rage*.

DEFINING RAGE

Rage sometimes behaves very well and other times not so well. It sometimes feels like an unquenchable fire and other times is hardly discernable. At times, it acts outside the context of human law and decency. At other times, it incites people to take stands for just and moral causes. Before we understand the *what* about rage, we must ponder the *why* about it. Listen to one woman's story that sheds some light on what rage is all about.

"Last week I had breakfast with a friend I'd been looking forward to seeing. Listening to her latest experiences and lessons was always fascinating, and I knew I could talk about the many things that were on my mind. I'd been needing someone to talk to. We spent the first two hours in deep dialogue about her life. I gave my usual sterling insights and advice and was just poised to launch into a monologue about my own struggles and discoveries of the past weeks when she checked her watch and hurriedly informed me she was nearly late for her next appointment.

"'I'm sorry I've got to run,' she said with a quick smile. 'It seems like I always do all the talking and we never get around to what's going on with you.'

"Inside I felt disappointed, hurt, dismissed, lonely, and angry. I needed some attention from a loving friend, and she was gathering her belongings in a hasty retreat.

"I was bitter, but I quickly put on a happy face and assured her that all was fine with me, no problem that she was in a hurry, it was great to be with her, hope everything gets better and better, see you later, have a great day, smile, wave, laugh . . .

"I was alone, again, and the only clear thoughts I had were, 'I shouldn't have expected anything from her. I need to tend to my own needs, not depend on someone else. Next time I feel needy, I'm going to make sure I don't have plans with someone who talks so much. I guess I'll go run some errands and try to forget about these depressing feelings. It doesn't do any good to feel sorry for myself anyway. Just got to get on with life and loving other people instead of worrying about myself.'"

How do you respond to the loss of something you want, need, or hope for? Do you throw a temper tantrum? Pout? Buck up and smile sweetly? Retreat into shameful isolation? Lose yourself and your feelings in compulsive behaviors? Snarl with cynicism about the crummy world in which you live?

Planning Escape Routes

All of these, and more, are the faces of rage. They are the escape routes from dealing with our real feelings connected with real losses, no matter how "insignificant." Over a lifetime, our escape routes become so well worn that we rush down them without a thought. We never stop to realize that our refusal to stand firm and deal responsibly with reality keeps us on the run. When we spend our lives consciously or unconsciously avoiding loss, we aren't available for meaningful relationships—not with others, ourselves, or even God.

In essence, rage is a self-protective shield we use to avoid loss-threatening circumstances or events. It gives us a false sense of control as it distances us from the natural and healthy emotions connected to past or potential significant losses that seem unmanageable. It is empowered by vows we make around our buried losses to ensure we won't be trapped by them again. It is grounded in self-reliance and a fierce or subtle determination to make our lives "work" without humble, childlike dependence on a God we don't trust.

Suppressing Emotions

Rage's sole purpose is to keep us from resolving loss, which would free us to love and experience life in the present. When we deny our losses or refuse to go through the grief process to resolution, we suppress our natural emotions. In turn, we develop a need for a force stronger than our emotions to hold our authentic feelings back. The only force strong enough is rage.

Rage is like a dam that holds back our feelings and hides our losses. The result: loss goes unresolved and painful emotions connected with loss are restrained and contained behind rage's wall. The higher the waters of unresolved loss, the stronger and higher our dam. Rage not only closes the door on the reality of loss and our need for a Protector strong enough to walk us through our grief, but also eliminates the potential for rich living and loving in an imperfect and often hostile world.

The fact that we can all point to events of loss in our lives is undeniable. How did we resolve those losses? That's the million dollar question. Did we grieve them fully or did we press on with life only to find them stubbornly holding us back? Did we apply an "appropriate" antidote, carefully choose a pat answer? Or did we fully allow our pain to precipitate the torrential "whys" upon our vulnerable heads?

The answer is important because if we habitually deny our losses by resisting the potent emotions connected to them, chances are that we are sitting on a powder keg of rage that will either explode or implode. At the very least, it will keep us from deeply connecting with others, God, and ourselves.

If we are to make any progress toward resolving our losses and subsequently relinquishing rage's stronghold, we must correctly identify our losses and understand their impact on us. Let's begin by looking at loss on two planes—how we experience it and how we come to interpret what we have experienced.

EXPERIENCING LOSS

We experience loss through either *abandonment* or *engulfment*. We interpret loss through lenses of either *idealism* or *realism*. Who is or is not there for us while experiencing loss greatly determines where we find ourselves on the extremes on each plane.

Abandonment

Susie's mother died when she was eleven. She was not told that her mother was sick with lupus, an incurable disease. She knew that something was wrong, but when she asked, her mother would just say, "I'm tired and need to rest." She would ask Susie to play quietly or go outside.

Susie's father drove a truck and sometimes spent weeks away from home. When he was home, he spent every moment with his wife. Susie could hear them from behind the bedroom door talking quietly. Sometimes she could hear her mother cry.

Susie was afraid to ask her dad what was wrong with her mom. He seemed so sad all the time. Finally one night, he told her that her mother was very sick and had to be taken to the hospital. Her grandmother came to stay with her, but Susie was not allowed to go see her mother. The adults told her that hospitals weren't places for children and that her mother couldn't have visitors around who might give her a cold or other germs.

One night, Susie was awakened in the middle of the night. This time it was her grandmother. She told her that her mother had passed away. Susie didn't know exactly what that meant, but she knew it wasn't good. She was told to be strong and not to cry, since crying wouldn't bring her mother back or make things any better.

The funeral was open-casket. It was the first time she had seen her mother in over a month. She didn't fully understand death. She saw people standing at the coffin, crying, and talking to her mother. When she went to look inside, she had a feeling of terror. It didn't seem to look like her mother. Her father was with her and moved her away, quickly sitting her down next to him in the pew. He never spoke of her mother again, and Susie's grandmother came to live with them until Susie was grown and gone.

Abandonment is the loss of another. The degree of abandonment is largely dependent upon the degree and permanence of the loss. Susie's experience reflects several forms of abandonment. Her mother's death represented total loss to Susie. Her father's bereavement and inability to communicate represented another kind of abandoning loss. Her grandmother's realism and ignorance about Susie's internal crisis was yet another form of abandonment. Simply put, Susie experienced a lot of abandonment early in life.

Engulfment

While abandonment is the loss of another, engulfment is the loss of self. We lose ourselves when we lose our ability to establish and maintain the separation between our internal and external worlds. Engulfment occurs when we are overstimulated, overwhelmed, overexposed, or overpowered by external circumstances. As with abandonment, there are engulfing events (e.g., witnessing something sudden, horrible, and traumatic) as well as engulfing environments (e.g., living with a smothering parent who is excessively demanding, protective, fearful, or manipulatively "loving").

Extreme engulfment crushes, more than smothers. Engulfing personalities are typically intrusive and often violating. While engulfment often occurs as overt abuse or violence, it can also be much more subtle. Engulfing personalities have no deep sense of someone else's need for autonomy and, therefore, are unable to nurture or respect it.

Not everyone experiences engulfment to the extent that his or her autonomy is irretrievably absorbed. It does, however, happen to too many people. Engulfment tears the hull of a person's spirit and soul. Unable to resist the torrential onslaught, these people sink slowly into a violent sea of circumstance.

Susie's unresolved experience of abandonment early in life affected her style of relating as she became an adult. Let's open another window on Susie's life, years later as the parent of her own daughter, Chris.

When Susie became a mother, she was determined to protect her children. Much of that determination was unconsciously rooted in the tremendous sense of abandonment and fear she felt while watching her mother die years before. To the child part of Susie, the unknown was terrifying and confusing. To the adult part of Susie, the unknown was intolerable. Susie had to know everything and would not rest until she felt satisfied in her pursuit.

Susie's protectiveness, rooted in her own need to resolve her long-forgotten terror and confusion, smothered those she loved and for whom she felt responsible. Her daughter was the most tightly wrapped in that blanket of protection.

When Chris was twelve, she became ill. Her illness left her hospitalized for several weeks until doctors finally discovered that she had a rare form of leukemia. The ordeal lasted for almost one year and included daily visits to doctors, hospitals, and cancer support groups. By the time Susie shared her story with our group, Chris was fifteen years old and had been in remission for two years.

While the illness was no longer an "issue," the relationship between Susie and Chris was. Susie had been dedicated to protecting her daughter long before Chris became ill. Since the illness, Susie's need to be involved in caring for Chris became an obsession. She watched her like a hawk. If there was any hint of a sniffle or headache, Susie reacted as if Chris were in a life-threatening situation.

If Susie were reading this book, she would never identify herself as being overly protective or obsessively concerned. If someone were to suggest that she was engulfing her daughter, she would be aghast. She would likely protest any further effort to point to the smothering aspects of her love for Chris. Unable to hear her own words, Susie misses the real root of her vigilant "love" when she argues, "Chris needs me. Her cancer caught us all off guard and she nearly died. If I had been able to see it sooner, she might not have gotten as sick as she did. I almost lost her once. I won't let anything get by me again."

Can you picture a young Susie sitting outside her mother's bedroom door, straining to understand the muffled voices and mysterious sobs? She knew something terrible was happening on the other side of that door and felt helpless not knowing what it was. She somehow told herself she must never be on the outside of anyone's door again. If there was going to be drama in the future, she was going to be the director.

When Chris became ill, Susie's inner vow called her into service to somehow control the inevitable loss associated with death and reverse its effect. Susie's need to be involved with Chris's illness ultimately mushroomed into an involvement with every detail of Chris's life. By the time Chris was fifteen, every detail in her life was scrutinized and monitored for the one germ that might prove fatal. This is engulfment in every sense of the word.

The Fine Line
The relationship between abandonment and engulfment can be confusing. Since they appear to be extremes on the scale, it would stand to reason that one has nothing to do with the other. It's true that they are opposites in the fact that one involves a kind of desertion and the other a form of extreme attachment; but they are both sons of the same mother—loss.

When an individual is understimulated by his external world, he grows up with a sense of loss in his ability to connect with others. When an individual is overstimulated by his external world, he grows up with a sense of loss in his ability to disengage from others. If we grow up without a clear sense of how we need to be stimulated by others appropriately, we will not know when or how to achieve intimacy while in relationship. If we grow up without a clear sense of how we need to be left alone appropriately, we will not know when or how to find space while in relationship. In either case we will be deprived of something we need to achieve balance in our relationships. Susie's unresolved abandonment left her without an ability to be close to people without smothering them.

When you've been deserted, there is no such thing as "too close."

Unable to resolve loss, its effects carry over in the ways we interpret life. While we may have lived seemingly centered and balanced lives at one time, loss has a way of throwing us off course. We get disoriented, confused, angry, fearful, and depressed. We need support to recenter as we swing from one extreme to the other—anger to grief, fear to rage, guilt to blame, pain to joy. Without that support, we run the risk of getting stuck or, worse yet, completely immersed in our own well of despair and pain. Once stuck there, it becomes the balcony from which we begin to view life's play. No longer participants, we are now critics—disengaged doomsayers and prophets warning those still on stage that life is dangerous: "It will get you, and when it does, you'll be out of the game."

Events, both future and present, are interpreted through a grid of fear and anger. This interpretive grid is expressed in realistic and/or idealistic terms. Idealism and realism become the rudders that navigate us through the seas of abandonment and engulfment.

INTERPRETING LOSS

In order to resolve the loss of her mother and her own feeling of abandonment, Susie needed an interpreter. Who did she have? It appears that the only interpreter available was her grandmother. What kind of interpreter was she? Did she explain death to Susie? Prepare her for the funeral? Offer an ear to answer Susie's questions? Tell Susie that her sadness was real and necessary? The only thing we're sure her grandmother did was offer Susie two pieces of interpretive advice:

▼ Don't cry because it won't bring her back.
▼ Be strong (presumably for her father).

Susie's grandmother was not a hard, unfeeling person. She was operating under her own interpretive rules in response to loss. Perhaps her advice came from a cultural assumption: "Children are too young to know what's happening. They bounce back. The best thing is just to get on with life and act as though nothing ever happened." This cultural "idealism" says if we continue as though something never happened, then we won't have to feel the pain of the event. The loss isn't real, so the pain isn't real.

Susie's grandmother mixed this cultural idealism with her own equally erroneous personal assumptions that reflected her unresolved past losses. Fighting back her own grief with feelings of futility, she pulled Susie into her own interpretive view that life had to go on, and that missing someone was an interference to its continuance. In her well-meaning way, Susie's grandmother introduced her grief-stricken granddaughter to her personal "realism." This realism mixed one part truth ("Your mom isn't going to come back") with several parts rage as avoidance of authentic feeling ("Feeling sad isn't going to change anything, so it's useless"). Her grandmother's realism gave Susie rules for surviving loss but did not tell her how to live reflectively through it. That left Susie with no ability to tolerate aspects of life that can't be quickly explained or resolved.

As interpreters for losses associated with abandonment and/or engulfment, idealism and realism share the following characteristics:

▼ Both are dedicated to the avoidance of loss.
▼ Both are mechanisms rooted in belief systems that are skewed to the right or left of reality and biblical truth.
▼ Both distort the way we view ourselves and others.
▼ Both serve as umbrellas for lesser belief systems—truisms—that form behavioral patterns of

relationship that resist the resolution of loss and change.

Idealism refuses to accept real loss. People on this interpretive extreme might be termed eternal optimists. Realism, on the other hand, refuses to accept real hope. People on this interpretive extreme might be termed eternal pessimists. Caught between idealism and realism, we avoid bringing authentic hope to genuine loss.

The idealist wife whose husband leaves her may interpret her abandonment by saying, "This isn't what was supposed to happen. I was supposed to get married, have children, and be happy. How could You have let this happen to me, God?"

The realist wife in the same circumstances might offer the following interpretation: "I knew this would happen eventually. It was just a matter of time. I don't know how I thought being married and having children would make me happy. You did it to me again, God."

In the face of loss, idealists feel angry, fearful, confused, and determined. Their motto is, "I won't give up without a struggle! To the death!" Idealists are willing to die in order to avoid feeling loss and its associated pain. They cling to false hope. Rather than feel the pain associated with the loss of their ideal, they cling to it tenaciously. Any attempt to bring reality to these individuals is met with angry and defensive resistance.

Realists, on the other hand, feel depressed, rejected, resigned, and passive. Their motto is, "I won't try even if you force me to. What good will it do to try? I've done everything I can do and nothing has worked."

Realists often die in their familiar pain. This is preferential to feeling hope and the new pain associated with it. They have lived their lives saying, "No one really loves They say they do, but if they saw the real me, they l reject me." When genuine and authentic love shines n their direction, the pain is excruciating. So stuck in the interpretive trench of "things will never change," true change is terrifying to them.

No one is purely idealistic or realistic. In Susie's grandmother's case, she carried a cultural idealism that instructed her to believe the best way to handle a child's grief was to say as little as possible and get on with life. It was a form of optimism that promised the absence of grief with the presence of routine and structure. Although she embraced this cultural idealism, her statements to Susie were primarily personal realisms. In this aspect, she was more of a pessimist. Her belief could provide no real instruction to resolve grief, so loss became a predominant theme in life.

In Susie's adult life with her own daughter, we see someone who has developed her own brand of avoidance. Having never resolved the loss of her mother, Susie resolved never to lose again. As long as she can maintain a sense of power with that resolution, she will remain the rugged idealist—never giving up, always looking for the answers. But what would have happened if her daughter had died and Susie had lost? It's difficult to say, but I believe she would resign her idealistic hope to the pessimistic realism her grandmother offered her so many years before.

THE REAL HOPE IN PAIN

Is there hope in pain? Absolutely. But when either pain or loss are eliminated, hope is distorted to become false hope or false hopelessness. Idealism avoids pain and loss by eliminating the loss aspect. Realism avoids pain and loss by eliminating the pain aspect. The following illustration explains the difference.

When you go to the dentist to have a tooth filled, you ask for Novocaine because you know that the experience will be painful—too painful to endure without it. The dentist goes to fill the tooth, but the cavity is so big he has to pull it. He pulls one of your permanent, non-replaceable teeth. You didn't feel a thing. The only way you know it's gone is by sticking your tongue in the soft, empty space.

Hope in this case would sound something like this: "I guess I will eventually be able to function reasonably well without that tooth, but this isn't what I thought was going to happen and I'm sure going to miss it."

We can't get to hope without acknowledging the tooth's absence. That's loss. We can't acknowledge and feel its absence unless we are willing to let the Novocaine wear off. That's pain. As soon as feeling begins to return, the pain becomes evident—pain that might even be worse than the pain of the toothache that drove you to the dentist in the first place. The pain acknowledges loss: "Something is missing, gone, removed." It's physical: "I have a big headache and my mouth is throbbing." It's psychological: "I really loved that tooth. The dentist told me it would just need a filling and suddenly the tooth is gone. Every time I take a picture, my smile will remind me that a tooth is gone."

When we allow ourselves to experience pain, hope begins to enter. It reminds us of the loss, which always hurts. But the reminder of loss helps us clear a path through the pain to a new shore. When we get there, we will be different—so will our world. Hope helps bring us to acceptance.

Never ignoring or erasing loss or pain, hope teaches us to respect and honor loss. It brings dignity to pain. It makes us stronger, more authentic, and more understanding of others whose losses mirror our own.

When I look at the scores of people who continue to buy quick-fix books that promise to eliminate their problems and when I look at equal scores of profiteers laughing all the way to the bank, it makes me heartsick. My hope is that those of you who read this book and are helped by its insights will pass on the unpopular, but true, message that there are no fast methods or easy roads.

The world seen through **rage**-colored glasses leaves out a great deal of life's picture. What isn't eliminated is distorted so that life becomes a cartoonish lark or a maudlin travesty.

WHY FACE THE PAIN?

Many people balk at the invitation to enter past pain and losses. After all, we say, those things happened such a long time ago. We survived and eventually outgrew the awkwardness. People may think we're too sensitive. Maybe it's wrong to admit and spend time addressing issues of loss that don't seem to be connected to catastrophic events. So why should we?

I can think of several reasons:

▼ To the extent we cannot resolve small losses, we will be unable to resolve big ones.

▼ Our failure to resolve loss will impair our ability to recognize and comfort our children and loved ones when they are in pain.

▼ Lack of resolution limits our ability to reach out as adults—even when we want to.

▼ Lack of resolution impacts our ability to feel and remember. Not only do we learn to block out bad times, but we have difficulty remembering good times as well.

▼ Lack of resolution forces us into self-protection that must keep others at arm's length. This limits our receptivity to the love others may want to extend to us.

▼ Lack of resolution causes us to project our past fears and beliefs into present circumstances. We may therefore mistrust someone who has never done anything to warrant it.

▼ Lack of resolution leads to the construction of rage walls that lock the needy parts of us inside

and deny access to anyone, including God, who
can heal and restore us. This dooms us to heap loss
upon loss until the fabric of our lives reveals a pattern of unresolved loss and rage that extends to
every aspect of our physical, emotional, and spiritual being.

Rage created by refusing to enter and resolve our losses
keeps us from wholly knowing, needing, and ultimately
trusting God. Our interpretive idealism or realism once
offered much-needed answers to unanswerable questions
surrounding loss. They brought us comfort and sometimes
relief. Avoidance is pleasurable for a time. It even gives us
a sense of power and control.

But the more dependent we become on our idealism
or realism to help us avoid or distance ourselves from the
past and to anticipate the future, the more trapped we
will be in our present realities. If we refuse to recognize
our rage and begin to overcome it, we will never find the
intimacy in relationships that the locked-up parts of us so
desperately want and need.

▼

CHAPTER 2

Eight Significant Losses

WE CAN NEVER FULLY eradicate rage at its root and, therefore, cannot eliminate its influence on our behavior until we allow ourselves to feel, grieve, and resolve the losses in our lives.

Many of the people with whom I talk have difficulty entering such a process. Their difficulty lies primarily in the fear of what looking at their losses will mean. When challenged with the prospect of facing their losses, people usually respond in one (or all) of three ways expressed in three kinds of statements: minimizing, guilt, and shame.

MINIMIZING STATEMENTS

"Compared to people who have really been victimized, my losses are insignificant. I really don't have any reason to complain. It's not like I was abused or something."

In this minimizing statement, one's own loss is regarded as insignificant in comparison to someone else's. This ignores that loss is loss, pain is pain. If you follow that line of reasoning, then the only people who would have a right to grieve or explore loss would be those who were the worst treated—for example, Holocaust survivors. And not just any Holocaust survivors, but those whose families were murdered in front of their eyes. And not just those whose families were murdered in front of their eyes, but those who were in the worst death camp. And not just those who were in the worst death camp, but those . . . you get the picture?

Victor Frankl, a psychiatrist and survivor of the Holocaust, confronts this rationale in his book, *Man's Search for Meaning*, by noting that pain cannot be quantified in such terms. He illustrated that pain is like a gas. If you allow the gas to escape its containment, it expands to fill the entire room whether there is a small or large amount.

I suppose someone could argue that a little gas won't kill you, but a lot will, and so quantity does matter if you happen to be in the room. I wonder how many of us are willing to be in a room with a little gas to find the line between a little and a lot. Frankl's point, as I understand it, is that people need to accept pain as pain without the disqualifiers that keep people from admitting that the one thing we humans share that transcends all social, physical, and moral boundaries is some form of loss.

It is dangerous and ultimately prideful to disqualify oneself from having to deal with loss because it isn't as bad as someone else's. I believe it's one of Satan's favorite ploys in keeping us out of the Father's arms.

GUILT STATEMENTS

"I can't look at these things. What will happen if I can't function? I have a job, a family, responsibilities. I can't afford the luxury of wallowing around in self-pity. Besides, those things happened a long time ago."

In this guilt statement, the person cannot allow himself the luxury of stepping out of his life duties to resolve loss. To do so would mean he would have to live with terrible guilt. Yet, he can't afford not to. In reality, he's not functioning very well as it is now. Sure, he's going to work, fixing dinner, and doing what he must to survive, but look at the costs. Look at how much energy he's spending to avoid feeling his pain.

It's not getting any easier either. It's more difficult for him to put on that uniform to go onto the playing field. If he doesn't address these issues now, he will have to face them later, and the longer he waits, the longer it will take to resolve them.

As for self-pity, a significant difference exists between self-pity and grief. Self-pity refuses to accept loss. It demands, "Why do things have to be the way they are? Why can't things be different?" It then adds, "Things will never change; it's hopeless." Self-pity invites hopelessness and bitterness.

Grief, on the other hand, can see beyond circumstances. We give dignity to our pain by allowing ourselves to feel and embrace loss. Grief invites comfort. Remember Jesus' words, "Blessed are those who mourn, for they will be comforted" (Matthew 5:4).

SHAME STATEMENTS

"The Bible tells me the past is the past and that I need to forget it and move on. I should be further along than this by now."

I hear this shame statement a lot from Christians. They maintain that if they were only more spiritual or somehow trusted God more with themselves, then there would be no need to explore the past. They somehow conclude that to explore the past is anti-biblical and disappointing to God.

Nowhere in the Bible are we encouraged to forget our past—to act as though it never happened. It goes against every principle of the Jewish theology from which the New Testament was born. Almost every significant holy day on the Jewish calendar and in the Mosaic law focuses on or around some significant, often tragic, event of the past. Even our Christian Eucharist commemorates history's most tragic moment—the crucifixion of our Lord.

Some people have interpreted from Paul's writings that the past should be left behind and forgotten. I believe Paul would be grief-stricken and appalled at some of the ways in which his writings have been interpreted. His letters are rich and uncensored as he recounts the many past events that made his life as an apostle unique and sometimes terrifying. As for his life before Christ, I believe there was never a day that passed when he didn't remember his former life. I believe the memory of who he was added to his depth of understanding and appreciation for God's grace and mercy.

ASK QUESTIONS ABOUT PAST LOSSES

Most of us do not have difficulty moving on in life despite a painful past. The difficulty comes when we refuse to acknowledge this painful past and its contribution to our lives today. I talk to countless men and women who say, "I just don't understand why I had to be molested or abused." "Why did my parents have to divorce?" "Why did my dad have to lose his business and our family suffer?" "Why did God allow such and such to happen?"

These people aren't looking for an answer nearly as much as they are looking for someone to meet them in their pain and respect their questions. We cannot fully resolve something we can't question from all sides and with full feeling. Questions contain our feelings and needs. They are part of the process of resolution—they indicate openness and vulnerability, reveal barriers to resolution, and contain fragments of lies that work to keep us stuck and hopeless.

When we are unable to review and question our past, we experience hopelessness, dissatisfaction, and guilt in the present. This leaves only the future in which to find solace. People with this mindset constantly race ahead with no ability to stop in the here and now.

FEAR OF FACING PAIN

Resolution of loss requires facing, feeling, and reconnecting with the part of us that experienced the loss. This is difficult and often very frightening. We didn't disconnect or separate ourselves from loss for no reason. Here are several of the real fears people verbalize when they begin to consider facing their pain:

▼ "I'm afraid I'll start crying and never stop."
▼ "I'm afraid to let myself feel the anger. I don't know what I will do. I might destroy something."
▼ "I'm afraid I will go crazy or that someone will think I'm crazy."
▼ "I'm afraid I am making everything up and, when it gets right down to it, I created all of this pain in order to get attention."
▼ "I'm afraid I'll get so depressed I won't be able to function."
▼ "I'm afraid my family will leave or dislike me if they see me crying all the time."
▼ "I'm a strong person. I'm afraid to feel weak and helpless."
▼ "I'm afraid of losing control and having other people see me."
▼ "I'm afraid God won't be there either, and then I'll really be alone."
▼ "I'm afraid of losing what I've worked so hard to

gain. I've spent my whole life working to be some-body important and needed. Now I have to need other people. I don't think I can handle that."

In each of those statements, the individual must lose a security he or she has earned or created in order to begin resolution. For many, the fear of losing that is greater than the fear of the original loss.

ANGER OVER FACING LOSS

Anger over the prospect of facing loss is as common as fear. Here are several of the angers people verbalize when the reality of loss begins to confront their own denial and rage:

▼ "Why do I have to do this? I shouldn't have to go through this. I didn't ask for this."

▼ "Why did God give me that kind of family? Where was He when all the loss in my life was happening? I thought He wasn't supposed to let bad things hap-pen to me."

▼ "I'm mad at myself for feeling this way. I hate feeling weak and depressed. I think I should just snap out of it."

▼ "I hate having to be here. I think I should be able to be better by now. After all, I've talked about these things before. I'm tired of hearing myself talk. It doesn't make things better."

▼ "Why won't God just give me a break? I deserve one. I feel like I have to be the one to figure all this stuff out."

▼ "It's not fair. Other people don't have to go through this stuff and their lives are just fine. I feel like I'm the only one who's stuck here. Everyone else is happy and fine. I should be allowed to be happy and fine too."

▼ "I don't have time to look at these things. Half
my life is over, and I don't have that kind of time
left. I need to get on with my life. You just don't
understand."

The anger and fear I've described are not tied to the
pain of the original loss as much as to the pain, guilt, and
shame of finding out that loss exists. We resist admitting
that life isn't what our realism and/or idealism tells us it
should be. Breaking down this resistance hurts—it is the
pain of disillusionment.

FACING LOSSES

Loss can be physical, emotional, spiritual, or all of the
above. Typically we think of loss in tangible, external
terms: "I lost my dog," "I lost my house," "I lost my job,"
etc. Rarely do we realize and verbalize the more internal,
intangible losses such as, "I lost my feelings," or "I lost my
will to live."

The damage from loss to our physical, emotional, and
spiritual selves depends a lot on how we experienced it.
Some of us grew up with tremendously secure feelings
about our physical selves and surroundings, but were
discouraged or shamed out of expressing feelings. Others of us were perpetrated upon abusively through bat-
tering or incest. Some of us have been attacked on all
levels, leaving no part of our beings untouched with
shame.

Since rage serves as a partition between our past
losses and our present reality, the only way to eradicate it is to allow our past to wash into our present.
Our losses in the past can be resolved and rage surren-
dered as our protector if we are willing to understand
our losses and how they affect the way we think, feel,
and live.

Eight significant categories of loss, if left unresolved,

precipitate rage: loss of *safety*, loss of *purpose*, loss of *significance*, loss of *authenticity*, loss of *eligibility*, loss of *hope*, loss of *dignity*, and loss of *power*.

✓ LOSS OF SAFETY

Tom was the youngest boy in a family of seven. He was an accident. His father had been sterile for some years—or at least thought he was. Tom's entrance into the family was not met with great enthusiasm because ten years separated him from the last sibling.

His family was rigid, and both his parents were extremely controlling and rule-oriented. His father was a grocer who worked from 3:30 in the morning until 2:00 each afternoon. He would come home every day and demand complete silence in the household while he took a nap. His mother was a homemaker and didn't rest from the moment she woke up in the morning until she dropped into bed at night. Every child had his or her responsibility, and no one failed to do what was expected.

Neither of Tom's parents was physically violent or abusive. Tom's father had been a deacon in the church for years, and the family was thought by all—including Tom—to be perfectly "normal" and secure. There wasn't anything inherently unsafe about Tom's home. It wasn't chaotic. He lived in a small community where people left their doors unlocked. Violence was something that happened in big cities and other places, not at home. His environment was as stable as any could be.

Tom entered a support group claiming to be a compulsive worrier. Whenever he heard something on the news about crime or tragedy in his locale, he became obsessed with making sure his house, property, and loved ones were secure. He refused to allow his wife to go anywhere without him. His children had to be home from school every day within fifteen minutes of the last bell. If they were late, he would immediately go looking for them. Tom's wagon was so full of worry that there was literally nothing in his life that he wasn't trying to protect and secure.

Tom's compulsive worrying was connected to loss— specifically, loss of safety. He had a difficult time understanding that. "I've never felt insecure in my entire life," he said. "It isn't me I'm worried about, it's my family."

How could Tom's compulsive worrying be rooted in a loss of safety, and if it was, in what way was he unsafe? After all, he'd grown up in a stable home and community. Indeed, Tom grew up in a stable home, but one with an emotionally abandoning climate. He always had an underlying feeling that he wasn't wanted. As long as he kept the rules of the house, his parents left him alone.

He thought back to his parents' lack of involvement and to some of the things he did as a small child. He shuddered when he talked and said, "If I saw my child doing some of the things I did, I would be a nervous wreck! I think I could have hung from a cornice over a marble floor when I was three years old and it wouldn't have evoked much more than my mother's anger over the fact that I was doing something that wasn't in the program."

Since his parents didn't seem concerned about his personal safety, Tom grew up feeling unprotected. As early as first grade, he could remember having an imaginary friend who was as big as a house and had superhuman strength. He kept that friend until fifth grade when he got involved with some other kids who were among the most popular and influential in the school.

A Universal Need
Safety is something we all need. In American society we are almost obsessed with it. Just take a minute to think about how much money you spend to insure it. It is legitimate to need to feel and be safe. When something happens to interfere with our safety, we typically respond with fear, anger, or both. The intensity of the response depends

a lot on the degree to which we feel threatened.

Sometimes our safety is deliberately taken away. Other times, we are the victim of unfortunate circumstance. Still other times, we find ourselves in relationships where those in authority (i.e., parents) have little or no concept of safety. We are therefore subject to circumstances that are extremely dangerous without really knowing any other reality.

In Tom's case, safety (or the lack of it) was rooted in not feeling wanted and important as an individual of intrinsic worth. His compulsive worrying filled his head and heart with noise and activity, distracting him from the immense pain of emptiness and worthlessness he felt. He hated to be alone because, to him, that meant being abandoned and unsafe.

While Tom's loss of safety didn't come in the form of abuse or instability as experienced in more chaotic families, and while his physical needs were always attended to, he was emotionally insecure. Since he had no ability to protect his emotional vulnerability, he became obsessed with controlling physical and tangible elements of his world.

Without a protector whose awareness and care extends to our needs for safety on all levels, we will experience loss of safety in some form.

LOSS OF PURPOSE

Reba has been married to a successful attorney for twenty-five years. She is a homemaker and mother of three children. For the past two years she has struggled with severe depression. She sought help when she began contemplating suicide. Nothing she did was praiseworthy, she concluded. She tried to convince her compassionate listeners that she was correct in this assessment by constantly telling them stories of her husband's fame or community accomplishments and her children's achievements. "My children respect the maid more than they do me," she said. "They don't think I can do anything. I think they are right."

Reba was full of pain and anger. These two elements combined to form a type of self-pity that was bent on self-annihilation. A part of her was saying, "Maybe if I kill myself, someone will be sorry." Since she could find no purpose for living, she became obsessed with dying. "I can accomplish more by dying," she said, "than by staying alive. At least my kids will get something for their future."

Reba's sense of loss intensified as her children got older and her husband's success afforded them greater liberty to hire other people to do the day-to-day cooking, cleaning, and household management. With fewer people needing her and few to no demands being placed on her time, she gave up. Her inability to adapt to change and maintain a contributing role in her family as an adult suggests that her present feelings were rooted in a profound loss of purpose.

We all need to feel purposeful—that there is some reason for our being. Purpose is lost when our attempts to contribute are rejected, scorned, criticized, stolen, or ignored. All children want to belong and contribute purposefully. Adults, however, often misinterpret children's attempts at contribution as a means of getting in the adults' way. For this reason, many of us have experienced loss of purpose at the hands of loving, caring parents whose lives are so absorbed with meeting obligations, taking care of business, and surviving the day that our need to contribute purposefully was lost in a flurry of do's, don'ts, exasperated pleas, hurry ups!, and I don't have times.

Often repressed or forgotten, such childhood losses tend to reemerge at significant transition points of change in the adult's life. This shows that unresolved loss is never resolved merely through the passage of time. What we begin to carry as children will follow us into our adult lives.

✓ LOSS OF SIGNIFICANCE

Martin told me that he wanted help because he didn't know how to relate to other men. He had many lady friends and preferred their company, but thought someone might think something was wrong with him if he didn't hang around with the guys once in a while.

I asked him how he and his father got along. He quickly responded, "We don't talk much, but I guess we get along all right." After spending some time with him, I discovered that he and his father had been distant for as long as he could remember. He explained that his father was a nice man and added that he never got a spanking or even a cross word from him. When I asked Martin if that was because he was extraordinarily good, he replied, "No. I just don't think my dad is the spanking and yelling kind."

When I asked him if he thought he wanted to have a relationship with his dad, he said he didn't know how. "I don't know at this point if I want one with him or not. I don't know how to reach him. It's like I can't get into his world. To tell you the truth, I'm not sure where his world is. Every time I try to reach out to him or make some kind of gesture toward relationship, he says, 'That sounds okay' or 'I'll have to think about that,' and then he never brings it up again. It's almost as though he didn't hear me, or he forgot or something. It's really frustrating."

Martin had always felt that talking to his father was like talking to a brick wall. He couldn't do anything to arouse him. It didn't matter whether he was good, bad, nice, or ugly; his dad seemed unfazed by his son's efforts to evoke some kind of response. This contributed to Martin's feelings of insignificance in his relationships with other men as well. It wasn't that he couldn't relate to men; he had just given up on making overtures. It was too much work and always made him feel bad about himself in the end. So Martin turned to women. He got his needs met in relationships with women and found them to be very appreciative of his efforts.

Just as we all need to feel there is a purpose for our being, we also need to feel that our efforts are not unnoticed or unappreciated. To feel significant is to feel visible, substantial, and essential—elements we all need to feel in relationship with others. When a child is born to parents who feel inconsequential, his need for significance is a foreign thing. The phrase, "Children should be seen and not heard," is one that does not recognize a child's individual significance.

Learning Significance

We first learn to feel significant by observing the reactions of our caregivers when we attempt to be visible. For example, when we learn to walk, we see everyone smile and clap. That tells us we're important and good. We feel attended to and noticed. Once we master walking, we combine it with other exercises, like reaching. When we walk over to the coffee table and pick up a pair of scissors, we see everyone reach toward us to remove the scissors from our hands. We receive concerned and disapproving looks. Big people point to the scissors with frowns and other gestures that tell us we shouldn't reach for scissors. Again we feel significant because we experience other people's reactions to our actions; we are not invisible. We sense that they want to protect and watch out for us, and we like the interaction.

What happens when we reach for the scissors and someone lunges forward, grabs them out of our hands, and slaps our hands while mouthing words that are loud, angry, and threatening? We, in our small child minds, won't conclude that scissors are bad, but that reaching is. This doesn't just disable our ability to reach for bad

things, but inhibits our ability and motivation to reach
for good ones as well.

Loss of significance results in a child's pulling away
from relationships. Interaction with important others will
lessen or degenerate to a power struggle between the child
and adult in which the child is labeled strong-willed and
defiant, or shy and withdrawn.

✓ LOSS OF AUTHENTICITY

I sat in a group one night while several men compared
memories of a loss of authenticity in their lives. While
each had his own story, they understood each other's feelings. Heads nodded and words flew as each spilled his
own cup containing memories of statements that, over
time, spelled out the rule, "To be different is bad."

Bob began: "I can't tell you how many times I heard
the words, 'Why can't you be more like your older brother?
He's so much easier to handle than you are.'"

Glen jumped in: "It's not so easy being the older
brother. Every time I wanted to try something new, I
heard, 'You can't do that. You have to be responsible and
set the example for your little brother.'"

Peter erupted with frustration about his church: "I
hate the feeling of someone staring at me because I choose
to raise my hands during worship."

Jeff told the group how angry he felt toward everyone
there: "I don't feel like you accept me because I don't use
the right 'recovery' words in this group. Every time I open
my mouth, I feel the tension in this room rise."

A hush soon fell over the room. I was thankful for
Jeff's courage and reminder that being authentic can be
threatening, even in a group of men trying to be authentic, because it highlights the fact that we're different from
others.

Shame has been described as the loss of our authentic
selves. Loss of authenticity occurs when we are shaped

and molded by the expectations of others who are trying to make us into someone they want us to be rather than allowing us to become who we really are. Authenticity is lost as a child enters the world of conformity and discovers that being different isn't always good or safe.

I rarely meet an adult who does not need to resolve at least some loss of authenticity. I can think of as many examples as there are people. Unfortunately, most people are not resolving the loss as much as they are exchanging one form of conformity for another. Without an authentic sense of self, we are doomed to an idolatrous lifestyle that is marked by huge investments in external and seemingly significant items and issues.

Often we compensate for this loss with militant individualism and assume we are authentic because we value our individuality. Truly authentic people, however, are secure in who they are and don't need a platform from which to declare and defend their uniqueness.

LOSS OF ELIGIBILITY

I remember the tremendous pain of being a seventh grader in a new school. Transplanted from a small town in Texas to a suburb of Los Angeles, I came to school one day to find the words "Sweetie" and "Silly Savage" penned on my locker door in permanent black ink. Those words were enough to tell me I wasn't eligible for friendship in this new place. I had been disqualified on the basis of a standard of appearance and behavior that I didn't meet.

Rejection, prejudice, and unfair judgment are the primary robbers of our eligibility, which is our sense of being qualified to participate in relationships. The kinds of statements that can contribute to a person's loss of eligibility include:

▼ "You're too fat to play. Besides, if we pick you we'll lose."

▼ "You're so stupid. Every time you open your mouth something stupid comes out."
▼ "We don't want sissies. Come back when you can stop acting like girl."
▼ "I don't want to see that look on your face ever again. Now wipe it off before I send you to your room."
▼ "I'm sorry. You're just not quite what we're looking for to join this ministry team. Didn't you say you've been divorced?"
▼ "Look, if you can't get it right, I'm going to have to find someone else. I can't waste my whole day helping you."

An individual who struggles with the loss of eligibility has a profound sense of inadequacy and self-hate. I often talk to people beginning to look at the reality of this loss in their lives only to hear them say, "When you see who I really am, you'll reject me too." Or, "Jesus can't love that part of me that was rejected. There's no way I can let Him see that."

It's destructive to be on the receiving end of someone else's prejudice or bias. What's worse, if we carry this loss without resolving it, we will make others the victims of our prejudice or bias as well.

✓LOSS OF HOPE

Terry sat across from me with tear-filled eyes, pleading, "Is it ever going to get better?" His previously secure world was unraveling at the seams—he'd been rejected by the graduate school he had been working for two years to enter; he didn't have a place to live; his father had passed away unexpectedly just a month before; his wife had a miscarriage after a long-awaited pregnancy entered its fifth month. Sounds like a modern-day Job story, doesn't it? Needless to say, for Terry, hope seemed intangible, unreal, and impotent in the face of his recent losses.

Hope helps us endure crisis. It gives us a picture beyond the immediate suffering and encourages us to hang in there. Most of us lose hope several times a day on some level—fortunately, not substantially enough to give up. Hopelessness usually comes when we find ourselves in crisis and we:

▼ can see no end;
▼ can find no friend;
▼ can exercise no options;
▼ can experience no rest.

When we don't have real hope, we begin to invest in false hope. False hope is a poor substitute for the real thing because it paints an unreal picture beyond the crisis. It sets us up for disappointment and feeds the tendency toward avoiding painful realities by fantasizing better ones that actually are not within reach.

Unmasking the immense hopelessness that lies beneath false hopes can be terrifying. This discovery makes us feel like there is no light at the end of the tunnel; we feel trapped and without choices.

✓LOSS OF DIGNITY

After speaking on the topic of rage on a radio talk show, I got a call from a listener who said he had a lot of rage. When I asked him to tell me what his life had been like, he said, "I was adopted. My father hated me. He told me he was sorry he'd gotten me and that he'd wasted his money. I was never a bad kid. I did my best to obey." He went on to describe some of the discipline his father used as part of "teaching his son to behave." One example epitomized the loss of dignity: "I used to get put on restriction a lot," the man explained. "My father would make me sit in the back yard on a blanket all day. When I came into the house to go to the bathroom or eat, he and everyone else completely ignored me. My father gave everyone explicit instructions to pretend as though I did not exist."

Needless to say, this man didn't feel valuable to anyone, including God. To have dignity is to feel our intrinsic worth. It makes me uniquely different, but no less special, than you. Dignity involves respect and acceptance. We are not criticized or shamed because we are limited and sometimes helpless. We are accepted and valued regardless.

Contributing Factors

A child develops a sense of dignity over the entire course of his emotional, physical, and spiritual development. This enables him to take risks and fail; to discover that there are some things he cannot do; to accept the fact that he is limited in areas where others are not and vice versa. Dignity is what prepares him to join the human race as a contributor to society.

A child loses dignity when he is expected to perform in a manner that is not age appropriate and then is criticized for failing. Other factors that can contribute to loss of dignity are:

Critical comparison to someone else: "Why can't you be more like your brother? He never gave me this kind of trouble at your age."

Failure to be credited for real achievement: "I see you got a B in math and A's in everything else. If you had studied for your math test instead of going out with your friends you could have gotten all A's."

Humiliation for having made an effort: "What ever made you think you were pretty enough to try out for the lead role in *Sleeping Beauty*? I'm surprised they didn't laugh you right off the stage. You should have auditioned for the witch. With a nose like yours you would have gotten the part for sure."

Generally, a person who needs to resolve this loss will display the following characteristics:

- ▼ will have difficulty accepting praise or compliments.
- ▼ will be very uncomfortable talking about themselves or allowing others to talk about them in an accepting or appreciative way.
- ▼ will feel that authority figures are impossible to please.
- ▼ will use self-depreciating statements.
- ▼ will have problems with promiscuity or will be involved in an abusive relationship.
- ▼ will be well liked by others and absolutely stupefied as to why.
- ▼ will be very apologetic and guilt-ridden, unable to accept genuine forgiveness.

LOSS OF POWER

Abuse in all its forms is disempowering. To offer one illustration of this loss is to exclude a thousand others. For this reason, I cannot convey this loss in a short example. So I will try to provide a composite example of a disempowered person.

Chris sat in the group, slouched in his chair. He'd been like that for two hours. He didn't seem to be engaged in or aroused by anything that had been said that night. I found this surprising because the group's interaction had been especially emotional and dynamic.

I tried to make contact with Chris by calling his name. He didn't change his posture; his eyes continued to stare blankly into a space known only to him. My only way of knowing that he heard me was his barely audible grunt that I interpreted to mean, "What?"

As I looked over Chris's application to the group, I noted a variety of symptoms that helped me understand him with compassion. It seemed he'd suffered from almost every kind of abuse known to mankind. He had been in and out of hospitals and treatment clinics for the better

part of his adult life, so he was familiar with thera-
peutic situations and probably resistant to what was
happening in our group. He'd attempted suicide three
times, had a prison record, and suffered from a variety of
obsessive-compulsive behaviors. He was convinced he was
possessed by demons and had participated in countless
church meetings where he was delivered from everything
but the kitchen sink—to no avail.

While you may not relate to such an extreme set of
symptoms, loss of power is most easily recognized by how
a person lives his life. Literally every part of Chris's life
was touched by a lack of control, purpose, discipline, and
meaningful relationship. To the extent that we lack these
things, we are dealing with a loss of power.

An Essential Resource

Power is the ability to reach out, explore, choose, interpret, risk, challenge, and perceive. It's basic to who we
are and who we were created to be. Power involves our
feelings, bodies, minds, souls, and spirits. It's the force
behind love, grace, mercy, and peace. It's what fuels our
imaginations, motivates us to create, compels us to nurture, and drives us to survive.

How can we lose something so essential? Whether
it happens as the result of a deliberate act of abuse or
ignorant neglect, somehow the plug gets pulled and the
lights go out.

Have you ever noticed how some people sparkle—
even seem to exude light—and others are very dim? It
has been my experience with victims of severe abuse that
their eyes say more than thousands of words. They may be
animated and expressive, but their eyes are dull, lifeless,
profoundly sad, and dark. This may sound sensational,
but it is the truth. When someone loses power, it is as
though the shades go down on the window of the soul and
spontaneous life is replaced with a mechanical one.

When I encounter people who tell me they can't

remember, feel, make choices, risk, hope, create, or imagine, I know they are struggling with a power problem. Somewhere along the line, the plug was pulled. People who have lost personal power often have the following characteristics. They are:

▼ extremely people- or substance-dependent.
▼ attracted to images of power—money, sex, certain kinds of drugs, politics, religion, etc.
▼ without ethics or morals in their pursuit of power when what they need to attain is threatened.
▼ unable to imagine themselves living without the object of their dependency.
▼ in constant need of something to stimulate and arouse them.

Having identified and defined the eight significant losses common to us all, let's move on to explore how we experience them in our own lives.

▼

CHAPTER 3

Five Ways We Experience Loss

HOW DOES LOSS OCCUR? Are we doomed to lose? Why do some people seem to have so much and others so little? How do we bring loss into balance with God's sovereignty?

Talking about loss opens a door to a roomful of deep and searching questions about life, God, ourselves, and the fairness of it all. They can be intimidating questions, but we cannot ignore them just because we cannot find answers to them. The questions themselves are part of the resolution process and, if given room to germinate, will prevent us from hatching rage. Questions are indicative of our need as people to reach outside ourselves for understanding, comfort, nurture, and protection.

There are five basic ways, or mechanisms, by which loss occurs:

▼ Unavoidable circumstances
▼ Irresponsible caregiving

▼ Lawless disobedience
▼ Social prejudice, upheaval, or chaos
▼ Generational sickness/sin (inherited family pathology)

PRIMARY AND SECONDARY LOSSES

Before we look at these mechanisms individually, we must understand that loss by one mechanism can start a chain reaction that sparks loss by one or several other mechanisms. For this reason, secondary losses may seem more significant and wounding than the primary ones. Let me give you an example.

I was molested when I was twelve years old by a stranger who befriended me on a lonely afternoon. For a number of years, I focused a lot of energy and outrage at that loss. The loss was lawless disobedience, the deliberate perpetration of evil upon another. It wasn't until much later in my resolution process that I began to explore the losses that occurred before that event.

Just a few months before I was molested, my father had left the Air Force, and we moved from a safe, secure military setting in a small Texas town to a large, suburban area of southern California. I, along with my family, was thrust into a new culture with which I could not cope. Because my family was going through a major transition that was part of my father's career change, I experienced a string of circumstantial, non-deliberate life events. My parents, dealing with losses of their own, were so absorbed in coping with the transition that my family went into a survival mode.

Also during this time, the U.S. economy fell into deep recession, double-digit inflation, soaring gasoline prices, etc. My father was attempting to get into the airlines at a time when they were laying off pilots. The societal upheaval escalated my parents' anxieties about the future, and my losses got lost in the storm of circumstance.

Unable to express my need, pain, fear, and confusion

over the sudden and dramatic turn in my life, I began to feel isolated and alone. When someone "nice" stepped into my world and offered to listen, I bit—hook, line, and sinker.

The circumstantial losses that took place before the sexual abuse were not deliberate—yet this does not and cannot negate their significance. When we are unable to resolve even the most benign circumstantial loss, we will be vulnerable to more deliberate and evil mechanisms.

If things had been different, would I have been molested? I don't know the answer. But I believe that the transition and upheaval in my family triggered older issues of abandonment going back to my birth-father's divorce from my mother when I was three. That loss had a role to play in my inability to adapt to the changes that were taking place when I was twelve.

CIRCUMSTANTIAL LOSS

I have already suggested that a number of losses are the result of life's circumstances. People being born, dying, moving, getting sick, and getting well are often unavoidable events associated with beginnings, ends, and transitions. Because circumstantial loss is a common experience to some degree, we have a tendency to minimize its importance and ignore the real pain we feel when it happens.

Circumstantial loss is not inherently evil or deliberate; however, some circumstantial mechanisms are the result of our own refusal to face and resolve other losses that may threaten us.

A typical example is the person who changes jobs every time the old one becomes unbearable or moves in hopes that life will be better in city B than it was in city A. In our efforts to escape legitimate pain or suffering—such as the pain of confrontation or the suffering associated with having our dreams frustrated by setbacks—we often set ourselves up for deliberate (albeit sometimes unconscious) circumstantial loss. The role we play in creating our own circumstantial loss is important to identify.

At the risk of making myself painfully transparent, I will use my present life experience to illustrate this point.

This is my first book. I cannot tell you how difficult the writing process has been for me. From the outset, if it were not for the encouragement and support of my wife, editor, and friends, I would probably have given up. I've dreamed about writing since I was in high school. When my publisher told me my proposal had been accepted, I hung up the phone and let out an exuberant scream. Then reality hit. What will I say? Will people understand it? What do I know about rage anyway? I have spent many nights in sleepless anxiety over the birth of this child.

This book is progeny, the fruit of my continual struggle to deal with loss and pain. The "birth pangs" I have experienced throughout the writing process are legitimate. Many times I have been sorely tempted to sabotage the task by inviting circumstantial loss to give me an excuse to escape. I never realized how good I am at escaping legitimate suffering, all under the umbrella of rationalization. For months I was faced daily with a variety of noble divergences that called me away from the lonely station at my word processor. Unfortunately, it couldn't soothe my fears and encourage me by telling me I was doing a good job.

In this case, my low-level conscious effort to create circumstantial loss is a means of avoiding another potential circumstantial loss—the inability on my part to complete this book. In this way, I can rationalize my disappointment and sadness over not seeing a dream materialize by saying, "I was just too busy helping people to get it done in time."

 We all have slightly different methods of sabotaging ourselves, refusing to risk growth because the potential for loss is too great. It's ultimately safer to stay right where we are. The part of us that carries unresolved loss often runs our lives more than we realize.

IRRESPONSIBLE CAREGIVING

Picture this scene: You're in a crowded restaurant sitting in a booth next to a couple with two small children. One of the children is about a year old and the other is three. The older child is behaving like a typical three-year-old; he has difficulty sitting still, wants to play with everything, wants to crawl under the table, spills a glass of water reaching for some sugar, and asks every ten seconds when his hamburger is going to be done. Add to this some statements made to the child by his parents:

"Do you want to go sit in the car? If you can't act like a big man, Daddy's going to take you out to the car, and we'll eat dinner in here without you."

"If you ask me one more time when your dinner is coming we're going to leave. Just be quiet and wait patiently. You're bothering me, and I'm tempted to take you home and send you to bed without anything to eat."

"You're embarrassing us. Look around. Do you see any other kids acting like you? If you can't behave when we go out, we'll leave you at home."

"The next time you interrupt Daddy and I, Daddy's going to take you to the bathroom and spank you."

"I'm going to tell Grandma what a bad boy you were at the restaurant. She might not take you out for your birthday next week."

"Jesus doesn't like it when little boys don't listen to their parents. How does He want you to act? What did you learn in Sunday school? You don't want to disappoint Him, do you?"

Since you're sitting in the next booth, you can hear everything that is happening between this child and his parents. If you're like most people, you have some specific advice to offer, and since you haven't been invited to share it with the people who need it, you quietly whisper it to the person sitting next to you.

How would you handle the situation? What would your message to the child be? What are the losses being suffered by this little boy as a result of the parenting he is receiving?

Before we become too harsh or judgmental, imagine encountering these parents in another setting. If you had a chance to talk with them about their children, family, beliefs, and dreams, what do you think they would say? Here's a sample: "We love our kids so much. You know, we tried really hard to have children, and it took us a long time to finally get pregnant with the first one. He's really our pride and joy. He's so mature for his age. He acts up occasionally, but really responds to our correction. We want to give him all the things we didn't get when we were younger. That's why one of us stays home. Yes, it's difficult to live on one income, but we really think the children are worth it."

Not a Deliberate Act

Is that coming from the same parents you sat next to in the restaurant? Absolutely! The point is this: Seldom do I encounter adult children whose parents deliberately and diabolically set out to ruin their lives. In some cases, the latter is true, but generally most parents try to do right by their children. How can someone working so hard to do right do so wrong? Once again, that's the million-dollar question.

To put it simply, we can't give to our children what we do not have. When starting support groups with adults, I tell them that most of us did not grow up with parents who woke up in the morning saying, "Hmmm, what can I do today to make little Johnny's or little Mary's life miserable?"

How we parent our children is not decidedly responsible or irresponsible based on how many mistakes we make in a given moment or day. Mistakes are part of learning. The example I gave does not reflect parental error as much as it reflects parental ignorance—not just ignorance about raising children. The greater lack of awareness in parents is in reference to themselves. So much of the parenting that happens in situations like the one I described is knee-jerk parenting. A child does something, and from some unknown and powerful place deep inside, the parent is compelled to react, often in ways that violate or cross his or her own standards. I can't tell you how many parents I talk to who follow their description of such incidents with, "I can't believe I acted that way. I treated him just like my dad treated me. I hate that."

Irresponsible caregiving is not usually rooted in bad intentions. In fact, the opposite is almost always true. Some of the most irresponsible caregivers have only the best of intentions. Those intentions are often verbalized in statements like:

▼ "I stay home because I want my daughter to have a mother. The only mother I remember is a maid. I felt closer to her than to my own mom."

▼ "I am hard on my kids, but that's because they need to know what the rules are. The world runs by rules and they have to get used to that if they are ever going to make it. I wasn't prepared for the world, and when I left home, I had a rude awakening."

▼ "We want to give our kids all of the things we didn't have growing up. Probably the most important one is a good Christian home. We grew up in alcoholic families. They were once-a-year Christians. Our kids are going to have better than that."

▼ "As a single parent, I am working hard to be both father and mother to my child. I can't help it that his dad left, but I'll make it up to him. I don't want him to grow up hating me."

Is it wrong to want the best for our children? Absolutely not. Are these statements inherently incorrect or misguided? No. However, within these good-intentioned parental vows are a multitude of unresolved losses, uttered in realistic and/or idealistic terms, that make it impossible for the parent to provide the care he or she so desperately wants to give.

Let's read the statements again. Can you hear the loss behind the good intention? This is some of what I heard:

▼ "I stay home because I want my daughter to have a mother. . . ."—the loss of significance, safety, hope, power.
▼ "I am hard on my kids but that's because they need to know what the rules are. . . ."—the loss of safety, dignity, power.
▼ "We want to give our kids all of the things we didn't have growing up. . . ."—the loss of safety, purpose, significance, authenticity, eligibility.
▼ "As a single parent I am working really hard to be both father and mother to my child. . . ."—the loss of purpose, significance, authenticity.

Much speculation could come from these short statements. It is important to realize that the parents speaking are in need of a parent of their own in some significant way. In their hidden feelings of abandonment, they vow not to abandon their own children. The first step toward responsible caregiving is for the parents to deal with their own abandonment and unresolved loss over having been raised irresponsibly. Only then will they be able to give their children what they truly need.

As I mentioned earlier, most parents do not deliberately set out to ruin their children's lives. However, many people have grown up with parents whose own emotional and spiritual sickness was so great that their neglect or abuse of their children had a deliberate aspect to it. Children in these circumstances are drawn into the parents' destructive cycle of avoidance, much like bugs are drawn to electric zappers on the back porch. These parents almost always have such a high degree of unresolved loss in their own background that they have retreated completely into a world of narcissistic fantasy. These parents abuse or abandon with almost no concept of the impact on their children.

LAWLESS DISOBEDIENCE

Loss due to someone else's lawless disobedience is often experienced from outside the family system, although children are often victims of the lawless acts of family members—molestation, abuse, etc. The victim is subjected to and often forced to participate in an act of evil against themselves or someone else. This kind of loss impacts society, making us feel helpless and outraged. These acts are as difficult to understand as they are to resolve, since they usually cannot be reconciled to our moral reason.

SOCIETAL PREJUDICE, UPHEAVAL, OR CHAOS

We don't have to look too far back in our nation's history to understand that societal prejudice can produce a great deal of loss to individuals as well as entire communities. When these losses are carried over time for generations, victims of prejudice can become perpetrators of their own brand of discrimination.

Prejudice of any kind is a disintegrating element. When we hold to our own prejudicial beliefs in any social context at the expense of the truth, we deepen the grooves of self-hatred and perpetuate a brand of rage into future generations that will be more destructive than we could ever imagine.

GENERATIONAL SICKNESS/SIN

Biblical texts clearly outline the cross-generational impact of sin. I'll define sin in this context as the illegitimate resolution of loss and the rejection of clearly defined biblical standards for relationship. The moment we reject a biblical standard of relationship—for example, love without prejudice—we step back into the generational sewage of family shame. When this happens, we doom ourselves to relive the same losses that we watched our parents suffer. The sins of the fathers are revisited upon not only ourselves, but upon those whom we are trying to nurture and protect. More will be said about this in the next chapter.

IDENTIFYING UNRESOLVED LOSSES

If we want to be free of the rage that keeps us from the kinds of relationships we long for with God and others, we must look at the significant events in our lives (past and present) and ask ourselves, "When did I feel a need for safety (or purpose, significance, authenticity, eligibility, hope, dignity, or power) and my need was not met?" We have to look at loss in relation to specific events and how those events impacted us.

A boy named Jimmy experienced loss during a two-year period. Though your own past may have been different than Jimmy's, as you read his story, try to think about some past events that have precipitated loss and how you experienced it.

The Pattern of Jimmy's Losses

When Jimmy was ten years old, his father died suddenly in a work-related accident. Jimmy experienced significant loss—a circumstantial loss. This loss was felt as abandonment—not just an emotional absence, but also a substantial blow to Jimmy's physical reality: no more wrestling with Dad, feeling his whiskers, playing catch, etc. The death of his father left Jimmy with losses of safety, hope, and power (figure 1).

Jimmy's Primary Loss
10 years old

Triggering Event	Jimmy's Reality	Jimmy's Significant Losses	Unresolved primary loss predisposes Jimmy to secondary losses that will hinder his ability to reach out and resolve past and present problems.
Father dies in accident	Physical and emotional abandonment	▶ Hope ▶ Safety ▶ Power	

When Jimmy was twelve years old, his mother remarried a man who had three children from a former marriage. The man favored his three children over Jimmy. He and his stepfather got locked into a power struggle in which they often fought verbally and occasionally physically. His stepfather labeled Jimmy as rebellious.

Jimmy's losses became more complicated. His mother's remarriage is again a circumstantial event. The fact that she married someone with a preexisting prejudice that favored his own children over Jimmy set him up to be the victim of societal prejudice at the family level. The upheaval and chaos over combining two families made matters more difficult because the rules were unclear. Jimmy's mother was irresponsible in her caregiving from the standpoint that she did not intervene to represent her son. In her efforts to make the new family work, she allowed her new husband to deal with Jimmy inappropriately. The primary damage to Jimmy was at an emotional level, where he experienced the losses of eligibility, dignity, significance, authenticity, hope, and power (figure 2).

Jimmy's Secondary Losses
12 years old

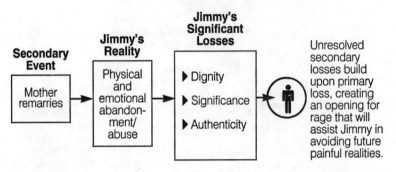

The secondary losses that Jimmy suffered were more wounding because they reinforced his feelings of power-lessness, hopelessness, and fear. Unless Jimmy gets some help in resolving his losses, beginning with the loss of his father, he will carry them into his adult life and thus interact with others somewhere along the interpretive continuum of realism/idealism.

No matter by what mechanisms we experience loss, the losses themselves are often more significant than we realize, deeply impacting the ways in which we live and relate in the present. In the next chapter, we will discuss what happens when loss builds upon loss to create a generational pattern of rage and avoidance.

CHAPTER 4

▼

How Unresolved Loss Visits the Next Generation

GENERATIONAL AND FAMILY PATHOLOGY is so complicated it could take up an entire book all by itself. This is by no means a comprehensive view of family sickness. I have included it to illustrate how loss and the mechanisms by which it occurs affect the family system and how the unresolved losses of the parents are often revisited on their children.

We'll begin by looking at Frank and Martha. We'll call them the first generation. They are already carrying a lot of baggage, which suggests that they are somewhere in the middle of a generational chain of dysfunction.

A LOOK AT FRANK

Frank and Martha have two distinct mechanisms of loss. Frank's father died when he was six, and his mother left when he was ten. At twelve, he went to work in a factory

and essentially raised himself. Frank obviously has profound abandonment in his life on all levels—physical,
emotional, and spiritual. Virtually every part of his life
has been touched by the absence of his parents.

His father's death was a circumstantial loss. His
mother's departure is unclear; however, we might safely
assume she was unwilling or unable to care for him
responsibly. Those primary losses exposed Frank to a big
and frightening world in which he had to protect himself
against the more deliberate mechanisms of evil and societal prejudice. Put simply, Frank's parental abandonment
predisposed him to face an engulfing world.

In Frank's case, his abandonment set up a cycle of
compulsive behavior (alcoholism and workaholism) in
his adult life that ultimately was engulfing. Work and
alcohol replaced the parents he lost. He turned to them
for comfort and found it only when they consumed his
emptiness.

A LOOK AT MARTHA

Martha's father was an alcoholic—what she called a
"mean drunk." He regularly abused her and other members of her family from her earliest recollection. Her father
was also incestuously involved with Martha and later her
younger sisters. Her mother became ill when Martha was
six and remained chronically ill until her death shortly
after Martha turned eighteen.

Martha was the oldest of five children, born into
an alcoholic family that made her vulnerable to loss
through a generational mechanism before she took her
first breath. Her father's abuse and incest suggest an
absence of any real physical boundaries. Martha experienced engulfment stretching through her entire childhood. The mechanism of Martha's loss was a combination
of irresponsible caregiving and a form of lawlessness from
within her own family system.

Martha survived the abuse by developing a well-fortified set of coping mechanisms (rage walls) that allowed her to physically and even emotionally detach during abusive engagements with her father. While these mechanisms enabled her to endure destructive evil, they continually forced her into engulfing circumstances. She couldn't relate in any genuine sense with people who would protect her.

It may seem that it is better to live with abandonment than engulfment, or vice-versa. The unfortunate fact of the matter is that they are complementary events. One leads to the other.

In Martha's case, her engulfment established a cycle of isolating and dissociative behavior in her adult life that ultimately became abandoning. When life started to close in on her, she turned to activity. She stayed busy from the time she got up until she went to bed. The activity brought her to a place of physical exhaustion that left her feeling clean and empty.

For brief moments she believed she was safe, which kept her emotionally distant from feelings of being overwhelmed, consumed, and overstimulated to the point of total overload. Activity was Martha's comfort because it consumed her anxiety. Like Frank's comforters, hers fell short of being able to eliminate the constant anxiety associated with the potential to be intruded upon.

A FAMILY PORTRAIT

When Frank and Martha married, they brought their histories with them. Neither of them could form a healthy relationship. Both were loss-ridden and damaged by years of neglect and abuse, making it impossible for them to see the root of their attraction to one another. Each had well-established and equally rigid forms of avoidance (rage) that made intimacy at certain levels impossible. So why did they get together?

Frank had never known real mothering. Martha spent most of her life being a kind of mother. As the oldest of five children and surrogate for a mother who was bedridden, Martha's activities were largely domestic. Frank liked the security of a home that had an appearance of stability and comfort. Martha's seeming self-assurance and ability to take care of herself and others made for a good match. Frank needed someone who didn't demand a lot from him emotionally and who could take care of his environmental needs.

Martha had never known a man who wasn't overwhelming and mean. Frank was nice, quiet, and even when he drank, very subdued. He kept to himself and didn't tell Martha how to manage things. She liked that. It met her needs for autonomy, while providing some level of security. Since Frank was not demanding or imposing upon Martha, she was free to escape when she felt overwhelmed without having to fear Frank's reaction.

While their relationship was far from ideal, their personal and family pathology made each the right person for the other—in a dysfunctional sort of way.

Frank and Martha started a family within two years of being married. Over a period of seven years, they had four children, Frank Jr., Mary, Maureen, and Frances.

Let's jump several years into the marriage and pause at the fourteen-year mark. Frank Jr. is twelve, Mary is ten, Maureen nine, and Frances five. For the sake of simplicity, we'll follow the development of Frank Jr. in particular.

Frank is emotionally and physically unavailable (he is always at work) to Frank Jr., who sees his father at meals and on weekends. They rarely interact or spend time together. Frank is transferring his unresolved father issues and associated abandonment to his son. It's important to point out that Frank would say he is giving his son something he never had—a roof over his head and some security. He would not see himself as abandoning his son.

Martha is fearful of men, especially noisy, assertive, or strong men. She is controlling and emotionally rigid with Frank Jr. They never touch, hug, or talk beyond the activity of the moment. Martha overpowers Frank Jr. much like she was overpowered by her father. She doesn't sexually abuse him, but she resists and shames his masculinity. She is not violent or abusive, but she is wounding because she will not allow Frank Jr. to exercise his own power. When he does, she is very cutting, critical, and emotionally destructive.

In addition to the dynamic between Frank Jr. and his parents, Martha has a strong alliance with the two middle daughters, Mary and Maureen. Frank has no direct attachment to any of his children. Frances, the youngest daughter, looks just like Martha did when she was little. She also carries much of Martha's personality. No room in the triad alliance between Martha, Mary, and Maureen exists for Frances, who forms an alliance with Frank Jr. that ultimately leads to an incestuous relationship that lasts four years. Frances inherits her mother's incestuous past and falls prey to her brother because of her mother's rejection of her.

A LOOK AT FRANK JR

Frank Jr. is now grown up. Let's pause to review some of the baggage he is carrying:

▼ His father was emotionally and physically distant.
▼ His mother was emotionally rigid and verbally controlling, using criticism as a primary means for parental direction.
▼ He has been incestuously involved with his sister.
▼ He carries his father's unresolved abandonment issues.
▼ He carries his mother's unresolved engulfment issues.

▼ He experiences losses of significance, purpose, safety, eligibility, and authenticity due to parental neglect.

▼ He experiences losses of dignity, power, safety, eligibility, significance, and hope due to maternal neglect.

▼ He experienced his father's neglect both physically and emotionally.

▼ He experienced his mother's abuse emotionally and sexually through rejection of his masculine identity.

▼ He manifests his father's passivity in relationships with others.

Let's take this one step further and look at the adult Frank Jr. as a husband and father. Added to what he is carrying as family baggage is his presentation—how he appears to others. Here's a short list of characteristics:

▼ He's quiet, but not detached.

▼ He has high expectations of himself and others.

▼ He is critical of himself, usually expressed through humor.

▼ He has to be in control of circumstances and can be explosive if things start to get out of control.

▼ He is moderately religious in that he has a sense of morals and ethics.

▼ He is a very successful businessman.

▼ He is extremely appearance conscious.

▼ He overeats and purges with several hours of exercise a week.

▼ He has a frequent need for sex (one to three times daily).

It really doesn't matter how good Frank Jr. looks on the outside. He is being driven by inner brokenness. With no ability to face or resolve his losses, he is running from the same things from which his mother and father ran.

How will Frank Jr. interact with his wife? What kinds of issues does he carry with women? How will he pass his brokenness on to his children? Each child will take on the unresolved losses of each parent. The manner in which each child internalizes and personalizes his parents' losses varies from sibling to sibling.

Then there are the factors of what siblings give to one another. Remember Frank Jr. and his sister? Sibling abuse and neglect in dysfunctional families can be as traumatic as that which comes from the parents. In many families, siblings are viewed as having more power than the parents. How will Frank Jr.'s children jockey to establish their positions in the family?

These are all questions that won't be completely answered until Frank Jr.'s children have children of their own. While we cannot answer specifically, Frank Jr.'s family pathology will be handed down to his children and so on until someone stops, sees the patterns, and resolves to end them.

I can't tell you how many people I meet in group settings whose primary reason for being there is to bring an end to destructive patterns of abuse handed down from generation to generation. Group members say, "I've been a Christian for a number of years. I really thought life was going pretty well. Then we started to have children. I saw myself doing to them what my father or mother did to me. I couldn't believe it. I swore I would never be like that, and yet there I was. I don't want to give my kids that kind of life. That's why I'm here."

AN OVERWHELMING TASK

Like the national debt, unresolved losses are sent to the next generation for collection—with interest. That fact is overwhelming. If we try to resolve all of our losses quickly so our children won't have to pay our debts, we will burn nd quit in despair. The pile of generational loss that sits at your doorstep can never be paid in full with your resources alone.

It helps to remember that Jesus stepped into the world two thousand years ago knowing that the debts were going to continue to pile up. We have His word and promise that He has paid the debt in full. We are free to go.

Perhaps the core of recovery is to reach a place in relationship with Christ where we can journey with Him over the terrain of our lives and see Him pouring the blood of His own life over the losses that everyone else ignored or refused to see. This is the only way to absorb the truth about what He's done into the fabric of our humanity so that we are genuinely transformed.

He won't go without us. We can't send Him back to do the job while we wait in our safely constructed fantasies of life. We must make the journey forward through the past with Him. That means we need to stop where He stops and discover what He's known all along: we have a great deal of hidden, forgotten, and repressed loss that we have been trusting rage to manage instead of Him.

We can't leap into the resolution of loss before we face it, and we'll have a hard time facing it squarely before we understand the insidious ways we have avoided it. In the next section we'll take a closer look at the specific methods with which we use rage to protect ourselves.

PART TWO

▼

AVOIDANCE:
How Do We Protect Ourselves with Rage?

CHAPTER 5

▼

The Deadly Dance
of Performance and Control

RAGE IS EXPRESSED in a variety of behaviors that share one important motivation—the need for control. Control mechanisms help the rage-possessed individual maintain a sense of value while covering unresolved loss and deep-seated shame attached to abandoning and/or engulfing circumstances. We must have control to minimize the threat of loss.

When the loss of control threatens us, rage empowers us to overcome the danger of abandonment or engulfment. We can develop highly sophisticated ways of maintaining a sense of control that use well-developed emotional and intellectual rationalization to sanction most of our surface-level behavior as "good" or even "righteous."

We've already discussed how we sometimes make vows to protect ourselves from being hurt again as we were in the past. Vows, like a pair of omnipotent arms, try to pull us out of our helplessness. Pulling ourselves up by our own bootstraps, however, is quite impossible, but we still try because we believe no one will rescue us when we are down and out. One of three pictures flashes before us:

▼ Picture One: Someone walks right by us without noticing we are there and in need.
▼ Picture Two: Someone walks by, sees us lying there and concludes that our predicament is not their problem.
▼ Picture Three: Someone walks by, sees us lying there and proceeds to list all of the precautionary steps we should have taken to avoid such an event. After dispensing a full measure of common sense, they leave us alone to think about it.

Whichever scenario comes to mind, in the end we are left to figure out a way to get ourselves out of our mishaps. Since no one else seems to care, we conclude that we must move to protect ourselves or else die.

When we experience helplessness without appropriate intervention, we suffer a tremendous loss of dignity. Our helplessness is ignored or exploited, rather than responded to and honored. We attempt to restore our own lost dignity and power through vows. In order to restore our dignity and power, we must mistrust and resist those aspects of life that have the potential to render us helpless.

You might be thinking, "So what's so wrong with that?" Plenty. Let me show you how limiting vows are. There are two kinds of self-protecting vows: performance vows and control vows.

PERFORMANCE VOWS

A performance vow addresses *methods* of behavior. The following is a list of some of those methods:

▼ "My father is such a *perfectionist* in his job."
▼ "My mother is so *cynical* and *sarcastic* when it comes to men."
▼ "My friends are really *activists*, they want to save the world."
▼ "My brother's church is so *legalistic*. You can't do anything but watch grass grow without having to be afraid of sinning."

Rigid standards of behavior develop out of performance vows. Those standards may be good or bad, ethical or immoral. Yet both extremes can come from the same vowing mechanism. Performance vows essentially dictate how we must act in order to keep our world running the way we want it to. Such vows are limiting in that we cannot live up to a vow like, "I won't turn in work that isn't the best," without being a perfectionist: "I can't make mistakes." Once we submit ourselves to a standard like no failure, we are confined to what we know we can do successfully. Change and growth are exchanged for the safe and familiar.

Performance vows vary from person to person, but are always rooted in helplessness associated with loss. To avoid helplessness, however, is to resist help—ultimately God's help. That's why our performance vows, even those that serve us well, must be exposed and confronted.

CONTROL VOWS

A control vow addresses rules for behavior. Rules help us see when we are stepping into unacceptable methods. We all need rules to help define security. Without them, we can feel lost and disoriented. When our rules become our security, however, we run into difficulty.

Control vows are made when someone breaks the rules and, in doing so, exposes us to loss. I have yet to meet a victim, myself included, who does not have a long list of control vows. The more profound the loss, the greater the list of rules. Here is a small list of control vows:

▼ "Always pay attention to every detail so you won't make stupid mistakes."
▼ "Never trust men for anything because they will always disappoint you in the end."
▼ "Never say you can't make a difference. You can if you try."
▼ "Never let anyone catch you in sin. Be perfect because that's what pleases God."

When we experience loss and its associated helplessness, our performance vows come first. We determine to avoid another similar event by correcting our behavior to eliminate whatever vulnerability we had prior to the event. Control vows follow as a type of parental voice. They pay close attention to every detail of our activity and flag characteristics that might lead to another loss. Once flagged, they offer specific rules for where and when we are allowed to be vulnerable.

Combining Vows

Performance and control vows combined work together to protect us in a fashion that sounds something like this:

"I saw a movie the other night that was pretty good, but I hated the ending."

"Really, why?"

"It was a downer, and I don't like movies with depressing endings. Movies should be happy. There's enough pain in life without having to pay six bucks to watch it as entertainment."

"I can understand your feelings about the world being a painful place. Do you ever feel helpless, like your needs are just too great to meet?"

"Once in a while I get discouraged but I just give it to God. I can't let those things get me down. I just have to believe that God's going to work it all out in the end."

Can you identify the performance and control vows in that short dialogue? Let's look at them individually:

"Movies should be happy. There's enough pain in life without having to pay six bucks to watch it as entertainment."

In essence, the person is saying, "I must be happy. It's not okay to feel depressed when I see something sad happen." His method of behavior is being "up" all the time. We would term him an optimist. When he sees something sad or painful in the world, his optimism protects him from feeling that pain.

"Once in a while I get discouraged, but I just give it to God. I can't let those things get me down. I just have to believe that God's going to work it all out in the end."

The person responds to the invitation to look at his helplessness with three control vows:

▼ "When you're discouraged get rid of the feeling."
▼ "There's no time to feel sad, depressed, unhappy, worried, etc."
▼ "Regardless of what my eyes tell me, I have to believe things are going to be better than they are."

The third statement is a combination control and performance vow: "You have to believe that God will work it out whether you think He will or not" (rule) and "Let God do the worrying, I can't" (method).

Do you think this person has loss in his life? You better believe it. His best friend committed suicide when he was in the tenth grade. He never resolved the overwhelming loss.

How dependent are you on methods and rules? What happens when someone has a different way of doing something or a different view of life? How do you handle situations or people whose rules and methods are loosely structured or inconsistent? Take the time to explore these questions. Vows are not easy to spot immediately because they seem necessary, right, sensible, and beneficial.

In my experience with helping people recognize vows, the first response to my confrontation sounds something like this: "Do you have to analyze everything I say and do? These aren't vows. This is just a scriptural way to live. God doesn't want us to be depressed or sad. Besides, I let Him protect me. I pray about everything I do and trust Him to give me what I need. I knew you were going to get Freudian on me sooner or later."

In short, the person responds in defensive anger. Vows represent strongholds of rage. They don't come down without a fight.

WHY PERFORMANCE AND CONTROL CAN BE DEADLY

Performing for others is a mechanism of control that gives us a method for fulfilling specific roles to meet specific demands (stated or implied) of those whose approval we seek. Without the mechanism, we have no way to protect ourselves from the potential shaming exposure of failing to please someone whose disapproval may result in rejection. When our efforts to control through performance "work," we experience a sense of purpose and significance—for the moment.

In family systems where loss is unresolved and rage has taken root, "love" is doled out when certain conditions are met and withheld when they aren't. Eligibility for nurture, protection, intervention, affirmation, and validation are predicated upon the child's ability to satisfy the demands of the value system the parent has learned to serve and trust (the system of control and performance designed to avoid loss). The parent will not permit the child to take risks or express feelings if those risks and feelings have the potential for loss that might mirror what the parent is avoiding.

As a parent's rage is reflected upon a child over time,

the parent's shame is transfered to the child, increasing the child's resistance to receive and contain the unconditional love he needs in order to resolve his own losses.

An Illustration

Perhaps one of the best examples of how rage is reflected between parent and child through control and performance is illustrated in the movie *Dead Poets' Society*. The film, set in a small East Coast boarding school for boys during the fifties, powerfully depicts the conflict between a rigid, authoritarian father and his teenage son, Neil. The father is highly invested in his son's future. His stated agenda is that Neil is going to become a doctor, and nothing is to interfere with that pursuit. Neil does everything to excel in his studies and meet his father's high expectations.

In one of the early dialogues between the two, Neil's father enters Neil's dorm room to announce his decision that his son must drop a meaningful extracurricular activity. It poses a threat to his studies, the father insists. Neil immediately protests, trying to appeal the decision. He argues that all of his grades are in order and that he can't quit because his role in the activity (the school annual yearbook) is central. His father interprets the protest as a challenge to his authority and vested interest in his son's future. He reminds his son of the hard work, sacrifice, and pain that have gone into giving him a chance to achieve something in life he never could.

Do you hear unresolved loss packaged in good intentions? The intense moment closes with Neil acknowledging his father's benevolent concern and apologizing for his behavior. He abandons his participation in the school annual and assures his friends that it isn't all that important anyway.

The movie continues to unfold the inner crisis of the boy as he tries to find himself outside his father's rigid parameters. His attempts finally lead to his auditioning ₒᵣ and getting the lead role in a play. After forging a letter of consent from his father to the administration, Neal goes on to prepare for opening night. Just before the play is to open, his father discovers his son's "betrayal" and demands that he quit immediately. Again, Neil attempts to protest. He pleads that the show is opening the next day and that he has to go on stage. With vehemence equal to the first confrontation, Neil's father rejects his appeal and storms away. This time the struggling adolescent does not relent. He goes on to perform.

On opening night, his father comes into the full auditorium as Neil makes his last appearance before the final curtain. Reality crosses the boy's face as he walks out on stage in full view of his father. Fear grips him, but perhaps he believes that if his father sees how well he performs, he will change his mind and allow him to continue acting.

Neal delivers his last monologue in the play while the movie camera shoots between his face and his father's, whose expression never changed. Rigid, determined, and poised for action, he waits artfully, as if the real stage is one on which he is the director.

Upon completing his first effort as an actor to an adoring audience, Neil joins his cast back stage in a moment of euphoric ecstasy. What follows is an agonizing series of events. Upon being summoned by his father, the briefly elated actor becomes a sullen child. He is rushed through the crowd of fans and friends with his father's strong arm and driven home in what must be rage's most deadly expression: silence.

Upon entering his father's study, he greets his frantic mother and turns to face his seething father. In exasperation at what seems to be his son's failure to see the importance of the matter, his father announces that Neil will leave the school he is attending and be placed immediately in a military academy to finish out his final year before college.

In a final assertive effort, Neil balks at what seems to be an intolerable sentence. As he begins to mouth what he wants, his father explodes with indignation, which silences the boy to demure resignation. The issue is settled. In an attempt to find some validation, he looks to his mother and offers a last pleading statement reminiscent of the evening's memorable performance. Her response is spineless and helpless. The dialogue ends, and everyone goes to bed.

Moments later, the trapped and hopeless heir to his father's suffocating expectations reenters the study, takes out his father's gun, and shoots himself to death.

A "Normal" Occurrence

What made the film so tragic was that it accurately characterized a reality lived out in one form or another by countless individuals in "normal" families during that time period. A discussion of the film with many of the men and women in groups I was conducting invoked an amazing mixture of responses. Some identified so closely with the boy that it opened many old wounds and triggered a flurry of emotion. Others felt sympathy for the father. They felt that he was trying to give his son an opportunity that would improve the quality of his life. They saw him as sacrificial and loving, if stern. You can imagine the discussion that followed when the group members identifying with the son heard the opinions of those sympathetic to the father.

What an opportunity to discuss rage! And discuss we did. We almost unanimously decided that the father was dedicated to control through authoritarianism and perfectionism. It was more difficult to recognize the control mechanisms of the son. I suggested that he was not visibly as rigid as his father, which made it difficult to see the degree of similarity between the two. Eventually, we postulated that the son was protecting himself with idealism and some degree of sensationalism. When I asked the question, "Do you think the father's authoritarianism and perfectionism were driven by rage?" the answer was an immediate and unanimous, YES. When I asked the same question about the son's idealism and sensationalism, the responses were less certain.

The reason we had difficulty being as clear about the son's motivations was because we focused on the overbearing father who drove his son to suicide. It was easy, even for those who sympathized with the father, to focus on his behavior and judge him rageful. Overt aggression is almost always simpler to label than passive aggression. The father's manipulative control triggered our own sense of injustice, so we were behind the son's rebellion with the hopes that it would bring the father around to a softer point of view.

The Son's Rage
In an attempt to help the discussion group see the son's rage, I turned the discussion toward the issue of engulfment. I asked a series of questions:

▼ How do you think the son felt about himself?
▼ Do you think he felt able to meet his father's expectations?
▼ Do you think he believed his father had his best interest at heart?
▼ Do you think he sought to please his father because he loved him or because he was afraid not to?
▼ How was the father's treatment and action engulfing?
▼ Was the son allowed to possess himself, his will, his feelings, and his reality?
▼ Why do you think the son ultimately committed suicide?
▼ What might have been at the root of the father's need for his son to become a doctor?

After spending considerable time, we concluded that the father's need to control his own world made him blind to his son's need to have a distinct and separate life. The more engulfing the father's expectations and demands were, the more hopeless his son became about having a life of his own.

In a scene between the beleaguered student and his free-thinking teacher after the father told him he had to quit the play, the boy pleads for the teacher's help—a way to change his father's mind.

The teacher espoused individuality and freedom of expression. Earlier he had introduced the boy to a Latin phrase that unlocked his imprisoned mind and spirit—*carpe diem*, translated, "seize the day." Can you imagine the appeal of such a phrase to a young man whose life had been so regimented and controlled that the day had always done the seizing?

The teacher encouraged his student to talk to his father, to express his desire to act with the same intensity that he was expressing it over tea in the teacher's study. The boy's expression spoke volumes. First an appeal, "Isn't there another way?" and then despair, "I feel trapped." The covert effort to act in a play without his father's knowledge was not rebellion nearly as much as it was an attempt to find some air in a suffocating parent-child relationship.

The father's obsessive control was probably rooted in some form of abandonment in his own past. His authoritarianism and perfectionism were no doubt the mechanisms by which he protected himself against the threat of being exposed as worthless. The father's avoidance of his loss set the stage for his son to carry his unresolved abandonment issues as needs for purpose and significance. That led the son to develop the idealism and sensationalism that motivated him to perform in order to avoid his own loss of authenticity, power, hope, and dignity. The activities he had to relinquish were all ones in which he was in a leading or significant role. While the son did not express himself in the same ways his father did, he was possessed by the same rage.

The drives to control and perform may express themselves in many other "isms" than the ones discussed so far. With passivism on one end of the spectrum and terrorism on the other, there are dozens in between: activism, rationalism, fanaticism, egotism, masochism, nepotism, to name only a few.

The important thing to recognize about our mechanisms to control and perform is that they are symptomatic of a preexisting condition that has its roots in experiences of abandonment and/or engulfment. Each "ism" has a range of intensity proportional to the degree of abandonment/engulfment an individual has experienced and how dedicated he is to resisting the resolution of loss by reinterpreting it through some brand of idealism and/or realism. The drives to control and perform are always evidence of deeply rooted rage.

In the next chapter, we will look at another contemporary example of rage in action that will help dissect its components even further.

CHAPTER 6

▼

The Furious Battle
Against Powerlessness

SINCE WE ALL HAVE some degree of unresolved loss, we are apt to be dedicated to an avoidance mechanism that colors our perception of reality in shades of rage. The degree to which we see life through rage-colored glasses is dependent on:

▼ The nature, frequency, and impact of loss.
▼ The interpretive input we received: How close to the full truth was it?
▼ How dedicated we are to distorting interpretive input when we encounter a more truthful interpretation.

The faces of rage we wear are the product of the following three components:

▼ The state of loss-induced powerlessness.

▼ The act of loss-avoiding control.
▼ The strongholds of self-made safety.

Let's look at these by eavesdropping on a conversation I had with a teacher who is beginning to discover his own rage in these three aspects.

I started by telling him that in terms of power, rage is the antithesis of love. Love is the power to nurture, heal, and restore—it is life-giving. Rage, on the other hand, is the lack of power to nurture, heal, and restore. Avoiding loss requires avoiding both reality and deep, vulnerable involvement with others. Avoidance has no power because there is no energy or love in it. Rage, therefore, while it may feel strong, secure, and reliable, is actually a state of powerlessness.

Because most of us don't have a meaningful picture of love, we are hard pressed to gamble on its ability to restore what we feel we've lost. Loss seems larger than love. We therefore need something larger than loss to rescue us. Enter rage.

I began to tell my teacher friend the story of how I have interpreted loss in my life and why I have turned to rage instead of love for help. For most of my life and even at times now, I have feared loss because I can't see what my life will be like in the aftermath. I might be alone, depressed, in need—disabled in some way.

My record of loss in the past tells me that the pain associated with it is too much to bear. Long ago I made vows that told loss I was not going to play into its hands. Basically, I was going to control life instead of letting life control me. I've told myself, "If loss in the future is anything like loss in the past, I don't want it."

"Isn't that normal?" my friend asked. "Are you saying we shouldn't be afraid of loss?"

"I don't know if normal is the right word," I answered. "It is certainly human to feel fear and for fear to help us see our real limits. But there is a fine line between healthy fear that helps us identify real danger and 'carried' fear that causes us to imagine and expect danger. Unresolved fear from previous loss is carried into the events we experience in the here and now. Reality today is colored by old and unresolved fear, making it difficult for us to believe that the result today will not be the same as it was in the past. Healthy fear makes us feel protected, while carried fear creates feelings of panic or paranoia. The first gives us an ability to make choices while taking risks associated with growth. The second paralyzes us so that we cannot take risks."

HEALTHY FEAR

I began again, "In the first kind of fear (healthy), the focus is on growth and change. Fear interacts as a part of the process, helping us to contain, sustain, and maintain our own power to move forward in a way that does not ignore our real limits or the real danger involved along the way.

"I remember when I learned how to ski. I definitely needed time to learn some basic skills in a safe place before I was ready to risk anything more difficult than a bunny slope. Once I began to feel a bit successful, I was ready to risk more difficult skills. With each new skill, a feeling of fear told me I had never done this before and that I should be careful.

"A greater potential for getting hurt existed. But so did more choices because, by this time, I had accumulated enough experience to take the risk. I had the power to move forward to more difficult moves because I knew the difference between ordinary danger associated with risk (I might fall down) and inordinate danger associated with risk (I might die). My experience told me that when I took this new risk, I would probably fall down but I would not die. I had fallen a few times and learned it wasn't so bad. My healthy fear helped me grow to become a better skier."

UNHEALTHY OR CARRIED FEAR

"In the second kind of fear (unhealthy)," I continued, "the focus is on control, not change. Risks are associated with peril in which any movement is potentially tragic. Back to skiing. On one of my first ski trips with my family, my father mistakenly took us on a chair lift to an advanced ski slope. While I rode quietly up the mountain, I noticed that the hills below were getting steeper. I also discerned that the people skiing down those hills were faster and more skilled than the people I had been skiing with all day. I began to feel panic, but told myself that my father must know what he was doing and that there was probably an easy way down. After all, he knew this was my first day.

"When the chair finally let us off at the top, I realized there was no easy way down. People were whizzing by me at what seemed like a hundred miles an hour. I looked at my father who, by this time, realized what he had done. We had to try to get down one way or another. As my father started slowly down the hill followed by the rest of my terrified family, I discovered that my legs were frozen. Not from cold, but from terror. I couldn't move. All I heard inside my head was, 'You're going to die.'

"In my paralysis, many irrational thoughts came to mind. I saw myself sitting on my skis and sliding down. It was too steep for that. I thought about asking someone to put me back on the lift. I thought about living the rest of my life there on that spot. I thought about what I would say to my dad if and when I got down safely. I stood there for what seemed like an eternity. I obviously did get down (I'm glad nobody took pictures) and survived to write about it, but the risk and difficulty were so great that I didn't learn anything from that experience except that I never wanted to do it again.

"I spent the rest of the day on bunny slopes that were much easier than the ones I had been skiing before the 'terror at the top' experience. It took a long time for me to recover from the loss of safety I experienced that day. Even after I got back to the docile bunny slopes, I still carried the fear and paralysis I felt while standing at the top of the world. In some ways, I had to start over to rebuild my trust and once again feel safe enough to take another risk."

The teacher nodded: "So you're saying that if we are exposed to overwhelming circumstances with no experience to navigate through them, we'll come away from the experience vowing never to allow it again?"

"Yes. We will refuse to take risks where the potential exists for us to lose control. As long as we believe we are in control, we don't have to be or feel powerless."

I had him hooked. I could see the wheels in his mind spinning, full of questions.

"So if rage is a state of powerlessness," he asked, "how can I determine whether I qualify? I don't feel powerless, and I take risks."

Understandably, life is not as simple as learning to ski, and while the analogy explained the difference between two kinds of fear, this guy was going to need a while to transfer that illustration to his day-to-day world. If anyone had it all together, he did.

IDENTIFYING LOSS-INDUCED POWERLESSNESS

I went on, "You need to ask yourself a few questions: What do you do when you begin to think you're losing control? Can you remember losing control at other times in your life?"

Actually I asked him these questions over the course of several meetings. The following dialogue is a summary of conversations that transpired over many weeks.

He described a recent incident at work, beginning by stressing the importance of his job. "I don't like to lose control there . . ."

I interrupted: "Tell me what you mean."

"Well, you know I'm a high school teacher, right?"

"Yes, a pretty good one, I hear."

"I like to think so. I work hard to make my class the best place for kids to learn. I am protective about my methods, and I tell the kids that while they are in my class, they must dedicate themselves to excellence. I won't accept anything that isn't the best.

"Well, one day I unveiled our spring project. I'd been teasing them with little hints for weeks. By the time I told them, they were electric with anticipation. The project involved simulating a space shuttle flight. It would be everyone's final grade instead of a final exam. Needless to say, the kids love that idea since final exams are always so stressful.

"The mission is to launch the shuttle and deploy a reconnaissance spy satellite. The crew also has a number of experiments to do while in flight. I've spent hundreds of hours preparing for it. I have plans for a command and control center, a flight crew, and media coverage. What's more, everyone has a part to play. The kids are really excited about it. It really is my best idea yet. It's in the final stages now. With two weeks until launch, I've finally got a bit of breathing room."

"Sounds like you've got everything under control," I observed. "What happened?"

"I'm not sure. I knew the game would be ambitious. As I said, I've done a lot of research. The other teachers in the school warned me that I might be biting off more than I could chew. I didn't pay much attention to them. They've always been jealous of me anyway. I make them look bad because my classes are always the first to fill up on registration day. I can't help it if I like to teach."

Refusal of Help

He continued, "One of the other science teachers who almost never says a word to me stopped me in the hall one day. He said he'd heard from some of the students about our simulation game and offered to help me out with some of the preparation. He also suggested that we join classes with his and make it a team effort."

"What did you say?"

"I thanked him, kind of coldly, and walked away saying to myself, 'That will be the day when I share my project with someone else's class. Let him do his own simulation game.' He approached me one more time in the following week, and I politely refused his help, telling him I thought it would make things too complicated to try to join forces now. He appealed, saying he thought I would have difficulty pulling it off due to the complexity of the game. That really burned me. Since when has he been so concerned? I smiled and thanked him for his concern, but inside I was fuming. I can remember thinking, 'I'll show you. We'll see who can pull what off.' I took his statement as a challenge."

"Do you think it was meant to be a challenge?"

"I don't know. He doesn't strike me as being the competitive or confrontational type. He's very quiet, keeps to himself most of the time. He's been with the school for a long time, so he stays busy with his own things. He chairs the science fair each year, coordinates field trips, and helps seniors graduate. I've never really gone out of my way to get to know him. We sort of stay out of each other's way. I get the feeling he doesn't like me."

"Why do you say that?"

"I'm not sure. I think I'm just too aggressive for him. You know, young blood in an old system. I challenge the status quo. Maybe he feels threatened."

"If he felt threatened, why would he offer to help you?"

"I don't think he really wanted to help me. I think he just wanted to get in on my project. He knew the kids were excited, and he probably didn't want to lose his reputation as the best science teacher in the school."

"I thought you held that title."

"With the kids I do, but with the faculty and administration he's still on top. I know it's just because he's been
around since the turn of the century."

"Do you think he's a good teacher?"

"I guess he's all right. I think he's kind of old-
fashioned. I sat in on his class while he was away for a
few days last year. It felt different than mine. Even though
he wasn't there, I could feel his presence in the room. The
kids were so quiet, almost afraid to talk. They just sat and
did their work until the bell rang. When I lectured, they
said very little. I'm just not used to that. It makes me feel
uncomfortable. I like my classroom to be alive and full of
noise. That tells me the kids are learning and interested."

"It sounds like all that quiet is a little intimidating to
you. How do his students feel about him?"

"That's the funny thing. They really seem to like him.
Some kids actually sign up for his classes before mine are
full. They're the real Poindexter types. You know, what
the kids call 'nerds.' He seems to attract mostly nerds. My
kids are more normal."

"For a person who doesn't seem to have much to do with
this other teacher, you sure do seem to know a lot about him.
Maybe he's more important to you than you think."

Going to the Principal

"That's silly. Besides, this isn't important to the story. I
was telling you about the science project and you got me
off on this teacher. I only brought that up because after
I said no to letting him in on the project, he went to the
administration to suggest that I might be in over my head.
He asked the principal to come and see me. That really
burned me. I couldn't believe the gall of this guy to meddle
with my project. When I realized why the principal was
there and who sent him, I was visibly angry. I could hear
my voice shaking and feel my heart racing and my face
getting hot. I worked hard to stay calm."

"What happened next?"

"The principal tried to tell me that he was on my side. Like all of a sudden, he's my friend. I said, somewhat sarcastically, that I appreciated his sudden concern since he hadn't visited me on the eve of other projects. When I asked why everyone was suddenly so interested, he bluntly stated he thought I might be in over my head and that I was taking on such a huge project because I was trying to prove something.

"He assured me that I didn't need to prove a thing. As far as he was concerned, I was a good teacher. I shot back angrily that if I were such a good teacher, he would trust my judgment as to how much I could or couldn't handle. By this point I was boiling. It was all I could do not to cuss him out and quit."

"Why didn't you?"

"I honestly don't know. God probably stopped me somehow. The principal left my room saying he wanted to see me in his office the next morning with the other science teacher to have a calm rational discussion about my project. He told me to go home, cool down, and come back to his office with a new attitude. I felt like a kid going to the principal rather than like a teacher.

"I didn't sleep very well that night. I thought about what I would say. I pictured every possible scenario in my mind. Each time I was the victor. In one scene, I saw myself stand up and point my finger squarely at the other science teacher while explaining to the principal that he was the one who needed the concern. I pictured the other teacher apologizing and agreeing that I was right. It's kind of embarrassing, but I had some real grandiose fantasies that night. By the time I went in the next morning I was sick to my stomach and tired."

"What happened?"

The Confrontation

"We all greeted one another with professional courtesy. I had a difficult time looking the other teacher in the eye. I was afraid I'd kill him with my look. The principal began the meeting by reviewing the situation as he saw it. He asked the other teacher if he had anything to add. He said no. The principal then asked me if I had anything to say.

"This was my chance. I was ready to go. I had the script all prepared, and I was going to walk out of there the victor. I started to speak and my voice cracked. That really embarrassed me. I felt my face go red and my hands were trembling. I felt just like a little kid between two powerful grownups. My mind went absolutely blank, and I couldn't think of anything to say. I think I ended up sitting there in silence for what seemed like an hour while they just stared at me. I finally took a deep breath and instead of arguing my case, I said I didn't have anything to say that I hadn't already said the previous day.

"The principal sat back in his chair. He looked at me, then the other teacher, then back down at his blank tablet. I'll never forget what happened next. He gave me permission to continue and advised me to accept the offer of assistance. He went on to say that if I chose not to work with the other teacher, he thought I would be making a mistake but he was not going to force me. That was it. The meeting was over. I walked out of the office in complete amazement. I had a great day after that."

"Did you decide to go on alone?"

"You bet I did. I wasn't the one who created all the fuss to begin with. I was minding my own business when all of that stuff came up."

"You sound defensive."

"You're looking at me as though I should have accepted the help. Whose side are you on anyway? I guess I am a little bit defensive."

"Do you think maybe you're afraid you made the wrong decision and now feel a little bit trapped?"

"What do you mean?"

"You haven't had the simulation game yet?"

"No. It's two weeks away."

"How are you feeling now that it's almost here?"

"Okay, I guess. I'm tired. It's a lot of work. I'm still spending most of my weekends trying to pull everything together. There are a lot of last-minute details to arrange."

"Do you regret not accepting the offer for help?"

"No. I already told you I was fine without it. Besides, you can't trust other people all the time. They offer to help but they end up taking over, and then they get all the credit for everything."

"Is that what you think the other teacher wanted to do? Take all the credit for your project?"

"I don't know. I've just learned that I can't count on other people. I don't work well with others in that way. I need to be in control of what's going on. I'm better at teaching other people to work as a team. It's been a good system so far. I haven't failed to do a good job yet."

Too Much Time at School

"Perhaps you haven't failed at school, but what about all of the time you spend trying to stay successful? How does your wife feel about that?"

"You would have to bring that up. I can't think about that right now. I have too many other things to do. She thinks I spend too much time at school, and she nags me a lot. She just doesn't understand how difficult teaching is."

"Don't you think your relationship with her is as important as your job?"

"Of course it is. I keep telling her that when this is all over, we'll take some time off and spend it with just the two of us. I didn't mean to imply that she wasn't important. It's just hard because she thinks I spend too much time with my job. Maybe I do, but I don't know how to do it well without putting all of that time into it. I think most people think teachers just go to work, teach a few classes, and go home. There's a lot more to it than that."

"You sound like you don't feel appreciated or understood."

"The kids appreciate me. It's just all the other people who think they know what's best. . . . Hey, I've talked enough. I was just answering a question about control, and I've told you my whole life story."

I told him his story so far gave a lot of insight into the questions I'd asked him earlier:

▼ What do you do when you begin to think you're losing control?
▼ Can you remember losing control at other times in your life?

These questions were intended to help him identify events of loss-induced powerlessness in his life. His story not only tells about his present, it lends insight to his past as well. It was not nearly as important for me to see his story's significance as it was for him to see it. It's clear by the way he told his story that he was resistant to any suggestion that he might be powerless. He didn't feel powerless, and he had an answer for everything. If I had attempted to insert my analysis of his situation, he would have become defensive. Any opportunity for him to discover the faces of his rage would have been missed.

Over the course of many weeks, I brought him back to some of the things he said, trying to help him discover his own resistance and avoidance to hearing himself.

HANGING ON TO STRONGHOLDS

Since I started by asking him about control, let's look at the obvious—his need for control and the manner in which he maintained it. When we began talking about his job as a teacher, I mentioned the fact that I'd heard he was good. I was interested to hear his response. When he told me, "I like to think so," he implied that others didn't agree. Later in his story, he indicated that the administration and some of the other teachers thought he was cocky and bullish. He said he had won the approval of the kids but was still being held at arm's length by his peers.

Whether this was true or just his perception is difficult to tell. I assumed that it was probably a bit of each. In either case, it was clear that he felt he had something to prove and was dedicated to doing whatever it took.

Dedication of that sort is usually rooted in deep insecurity—the feeling of being unsafe. Again, since he didn't see himself as insecure, it would have been useless to try to point that out. Instead, I encouraged him to reflect on his dedication by introducing a few more questions.

Perfectionism

"You said you work hard to make your class the best place for kids to learn. You also said you are protective about your methods and that you demand excellence from every one of your students. You finished by saying you won't accept anything less than the best. It sounds like you have some high standards not only for yourself, but for other people."

"Is there anything wrong with that?" he snapped.

"You're responding to me as though you thought I was telling you there is something wrong with that. I'm not making a judgment. I'm simply observing that you seem to have high standards."

"I guess I do. But that's only because I want what's best for the kids."

"Do you think you may be afraid to let them fail? Perhaps you believe that if they're working hard in your class, it somehow reflects well on your teaching ability. In other words, you need their enthusiasm and dedication in order to feel valuable and worthwhile."

"If you're saying I need their approval, I don't. I'm a good teacher. Nobody can take that away from me."

"That almost sounds like a vow. I wonder what would happen if they tried. It seems that your story is about someone trying to take it away. Back to the need for their approval, what happens when your class doesn't go well?"

"It's been a long time since that happened. I try not to let it happen, but if I do have a bad day, I can't sleep that night. The day just rolls through my mind like a movie. I lay awake trying to think of what I did wrong and what I need to do to avoid having it happen again. I go back the next day determined to make it a better one. Really, the only time I have a bad day is when I'm lazy or unmotivated."

"Do you get defensive when someone comments on your bad days?"

"I guess I do. I take pride in doing my job well."

"Do you think you might do anything to avoid criticism?"

"Yes. I hate criticism."

That statement brought us to a first step in identifying his loss-avoidance control. Can you hear the perfectionist in him? He's the kind of person who is harder on himself than anyone. Being perfect or performing flawlessly was his control that protected him against the loss of power associated with criticism. As long as he had his performance under control, he didn't have to look at the potential to be wounded by someone else's disapproval. Perfectionism had become a familiar stronghold where he hid from any threat to the safety of his soul.

In addition to the perfect standards to which he held himself, and in some sense others, he had a real power struggle with his peers. He mentioned one in particular, but suggested that most or all of the other teachers were jealous. He responded protectively by adding, "I don't pay attention to them."

Separatism

"Do you wish you had a better relationship with the other teachers?" I asked.

"Not really. I don't like to sit around and gossip. I don't have too many interests in common with them. I do much better on my own."

"You mentioned you thought they were jealous of you. That's a powerful feeling. Jealousy is usually something we feel when we're close to someone and our position in their life gets threatened. Do you think the teachers want to be a part of your world, but you won't let them?"

"I think the only reason they would want to be a part of my world is to steal my ideas. I don't think they really care about me. I think they would really like to see me fail. I'm just not part of their crowd."

"Have they ever given you any reason to believe they would like to see you fail? Have they ever told you they didn't want you to be a part of their crowd?"

"No, not in so many words. But why else would they want to have a relationship with me?"

I asked him to think about what he'd just asked. "Why would anyone want to have relationship with you? Why do you assume they wouldn't?"

"I don't know. I guess because people have always told me I was a showoff. They think I want all of the attention and that I'm selfish."

"Is that true?"

"I don't know. I don't think so, but then everyone always says it is."

"Who is everyone?"

"Well, it used to be my family. My brother and sisters used to say, 'Stop being such a showoff. If you think you're going to get other people to like you that way, think again. You're just a bothersome pest.'"

"That sounds like rejection to me. I'll bet you'll do anything to avoid being rejected by someone. Even if that means rejecting them first."

"I think I just told myself I didn't need anyone. I was always such a loner. Besides, I was different—you know, a bookworm. I liked asking questions and exploring things. My family thought I was weird. My dad was really critical. I guess he expected me to follow my brother's line of hunting, sports, and girls. Those things just never appealed to me."

Once again, my friend came to a step in identifying his own loss-avoidance behavior. In his past experience, rejection always brought loss. His way of avoiding rejection (which at the hands of his father and siblings came in the form of criticism) was to withdraw into a world where people didn't matter. To not need anyone, to "voluntarily" separate from others, was to be in control. Separatism became a perfectly reasonable stronghold of self-made safety.

No wonder he reacted so angrily to the other teacher's suggestions that he needed help. His belief that other people were jealous was his own rationalization for why they wouldn't accept him and, therefore, why he needed to stay separate from them. He, in his own mind, became superior, which facilitated his avoidance by underscoring that he really didn't need anyone.

In reality, it was almost inconceivable to him that someone would actually want to help or even like him. His statement, "Why else would they want to have a relationship with me?" reveals his own self-rejection and self-hatred—something he would not readily see for some time.

Skepticism

A final insight into my friend's loss-avoidance control became readily apparent. Skepticism had become a third reliable stronghold against any threat. Doubting others' sincere motives or intentions kept him safe from their involvement and possible rejection.

When he was approached by his colleague and offered

help, he became suspicious and exclusive. Listen to the mistrust in his comments: "That will be the day when I share my project with someone else. . . . Besides, he's not really concerned about what I need." Full of suspicion, he perceived an offer for help as a lack of support or belief in his ability to achieve something.

"It sounds like you need to prove to the other science teacher that you're as good as he is," I observed. "I wonder why it's so important to show him that you're good enough?"

"I don't know about proving something. I don't trust him. I don't think he's sincere about helping, and I don't like the way he treated me."

"I honestly don't hear that he's treated you badly at all. Maybe he shouldn't have gone over your head, but it appears he had a real concern, and when you rejected his observation, he felt you might be more receptive to someone who was neutral."

"I've tried to get to know him in the past. He's very quiet and keeps to himself. I don't think he likes me. I just feel better if he minds his own business and lets me take care of myself."

"It sounds like his quiet and reserved manner unsettles you. What does someone's silence mean to you?"

"It makes me very uncomfortable. It makes me feel like I'm not good enough."

"Has this teacher ever told you he thought you were an inferior teacher?"

"No."

"I wonder where you learned that silence meant you were inferior?"

"Well, my dad was quiet. Being the youngest of six kids, I was told by my brother and sisters that Dad was mad. Whoever he wasn't speaking to was the one he didn't approve of at that moment. He hardly ever talked to me. It makes me uncomfortable when people don't talk. I can't tell what they're thinking, but I'm sure it's not good. I don't like it when it's quiet. If I don't have some noise going all the time, I feel weird. That's why I have such an active class."

It wasn't hard for my friend to identify an underlying assumption that dictated his behavior—silent or reserved people are judging and disapproving people. Silence also triggered a deep feeling of being ignored. His father "hardly ever talked" to him, but at the same time was close to his brother.

Playing Favorites

"My older brother was his favorite," he said. "He did everything to please my dad. I was always in his shadow. People would say, 'Oh, you must be Sam's little brother.' There was Sam, four girls, and me. Dad called Sam No. 1 son and me No. 2. I don't know if he realized how much that hurt me. Eventually, I was as good as Sam at everything. Scholastically I was even better than he was.

"When I started getting on an equal par with Sam, he began to take an interest in me. I trusted him at first. I really liked his attention, because up until that time he acted as though I didn't exist. He seemed like he really cared. I let him help me until I saw what he was up to. He just wanted to look good to my dad. He always made sure Dad knew he was giving his 'little brother' a hand. My dad would smile at Sam and say to me, 'You sure have a great big brother. You should be thankful. Not many older brothers would take the time to help their younger brothers out.' Then he and Sam would go off and do something together."

As I listened I began to understand why the other science teacher was such a threat. Without even being aware of it, my friend was reliving his family dynamic. I pointed it out to him.

"You remember telling me that the other science teacher was considered the best by the administration?"

"Yes."

"Do you remember telling me why he was the best?"

"Yes, I think I said it was because he'd been there forever. He had them all brainwashed, I guess."

"That's right, but you admitted to me that he was a good teacher and that his classes were always full. Isn't it possible that he really deserves the respect and title given to him by others?"

"I guess so, but I think he's got everyone fooled. Why do you think he came to me? He wanted to get in on my project because he knew it would win me recognition. He was mad because he can't come up with innovative and new ideas. I think I'm a threat to him. It doesn't matter anyway. The kids all think I'm the best and it's just a matter of time until everyone else knows, too."

"Can you hear yourself talk?" I asked him. "It's as though you are having to compete for the attention of someone you really need. Do you think there may be any parallel between the conflict you're having at school and the one you grew up with trying to out-perform your brother in order to get your dad to notice you?"

"If you're trying to tell me that what I'm telling you about my job has something to do with my childhood, you can forget it. I think that stuff is, for the most part, some kind of psychological mumbo-jumbo. I'm grown up now. Not only that, but my dad, my brother, and I all get along fine. They think I'm great and tell me so."

"I can feel your resistance again. I'm not trying to force any view on you. I'm simply asking you if you see some kind of connection or similarity."

"I just don't want you to try to tell me that I hate my dad or something. I can see some of what you are saying. I can't lie and say that my dad didn't favor my brother. I'm just glad it's not that way anymore."

PUTTING THE PUZZLE TOGETHER

I asked him if he'd ever put together a jigsaw puzzle.

"Yes, when I was younger."

"Can you remember how you started it? Didn't you pour all of the pieces out on the table? Some were upside down, everything was in one big pile. It looked nothing like the picture on the box. Getting it to look just like that picture on the box took a lot of sorting, thinking, and trying possibilities. If you had picked up one of the pieces and tried to make it fit with another one because the shapes almost fit, you never would have been able to put the puzzle together. Instead, you had to find all of the edge pieces; you had to sort colors and shapes. This took some time. Only then could you begin to look for where the pieces fit."

He rolled his eyes. "So what are you getting at? Are you going to tell me my life is like a puzzle?"

"You're obviously smart enough to get the message. I'm saying that before you rule out possibilities and come up with an erroneous picture, take some time to sort through the pieces. You are giving me pieces that include pictures from the recent and distant past. Every piece fits somewhere. Not one of them should be thrown away. If we disqualify or eliminate a piece because it 'seems' insignificant, we are going to finish with an incomplete picture. It's easy to want to change the picture or say that because it looks good now, we shouldn't think about when it was less than good."

"Well, all I know is this thing with school has been really difficult. I guess I just figured it was because the other teacher was overstepping his bounds."

"Perhaps he was. Regardless, his action caused a reaction in you that brought up all kinds of things you're still trying to sort through. It shook you pretty hard."

"I can't argue with that."

I reminded him of my original questions about control and what happens when he thinks he's going to lose it. Before he could see clearly how he was devoted to maintaining control, he needed to be honest about how he began to lose it.

The First Piece

"It's pretty clear," I said, "that when the other teacher stepped in to offer support, you felt threatened and suspicious. Your ability to do your own thing and not rely on someone else for anything was your way of maintaining control, and that was threatened. When I suggested that the other teacher was more important to you than you think, you changed the subject and blamed me for the direction our conversation was taking.

"That tells me you don't want to think the other teacher is important. You may continue to deny that he matters, but the principal certainly does. Can you see how the teacher further threatened your control by going to the principal? Who is to say that the principal wouldn't have done just what your dad did by telling you how lucky you were to have someone so capable to help you with a project? In some sense, he must have agreed with the other teacher or he wouldn't have called you in to meet with him. You told me you worked hard to stay calm."

"Well, I couldn't lose control," he said. "There's that word again. What I mean is, I couldn't get angry."

"Weren't you a little late for that? It sounds like you were angry."

"I was. What I mean is, I couldn't let him see that I was angry. I had to keep it together."

"Was anger something that was okay to express in your household while you were growing up?"

"Are you kidding? Anger was forbidden. Under no circumstances did you let someone see you were mad. I can remember once getting mad at my older brother and calling him a name. I don't wear a belt to this day because the mere sight of one reminds me of the whipping I got for that."

"Were you afraid of the principal? What would he do if he saw you angry?"

"I don't know. I haven't ever been angry around him

e's pretty mellow. I guess maybe he would rep-
rımand me or tell me to cool down."

"He seems to like you. He said you were a good
teacher."

"If he really thought I was a good teacher, he would
have told the other teacher to get off my back. Besides,
if I went to the principal about the other teacher and the
tables were reversed, I doubt very much that the principal
would have paid him a visit—except maybe to laugh about
my concern."

"So you have a hard time trusting that he's on your
side or even willing to consider your side. It sounds like
you think he believes everything the other teacher says
and does so without questioning it at all."

"Logically, based on the outcome, I know he doesn't.
I guess I have a hard time really believing it though."

A Family Piece

I suggested that this could be another family piece to the
puzzle. "Was anyone ever on your side in your family?"
I asked.

"No."

"How did that feel?"

"It felt frustrating. Nobody ever listened to my side.
I always felt condemned before I could have my day in
court. My brother and my dad were always allies. They
just decided things for me and then told me how it was
going to be."

"It sounds like you felt powerless—like a little kid
with a world of big people telling you what to do and
what you needed. Now that I think about it, you did say
you felt more like a kid than a teacher when you went to
the principal's office."

"I did feel that way."

"You also told me you couldn't look the other teacher
in the eye. Let's say that was because, in some ways,
he was big and you were little. When one of your young

students can't look you in the eye, what do you think it means?"

"I don't know. I guess they feel embarrassed or self-conscious."

"Did you feel embarrassed or self-conscious? Almost as though if you looked at him, he would see through you—he would see how small you felt?"

"I didn't really give it much thought. I guess I didn't look at him because I didn't want to kill him with my stare."

I asked him to close his eyes and try to picture his dad and brother. "Can you see them?" I asked.

"Yes."

"Where are they?"

"Sitting in the living room. They used to like to watch sports together on TV."

"Where are you in the picture?"

"I'm not."

I asked him to try to put himself in the picture. "Where would you normally be?"

"Well, I'm in the room standing in the doorway between the kitchen and the couch they are sitting on."

"Can they see you?"

"Are you kidding? They won't look up for at least a few more minutes. Eventually, they'll head my way because they go to the kitchen during commercials."

"All right. I want you to walk over to them, pull up a chair, and sit between them and the TV."

"You've got to be nuts. They'll get really mad."

"Just try it. I want you to be in full view. Are you there yet?"

"Yes."

"Can they see you?"

"Yes, I think so."

"I want you to look them both right in the eye. What do you see?"

"They're looking at me. It's hard not to look away."

"I want you to keep on looking and tell me what you see."

"They look angry. I don't think they like me in their way. They look like they are waiting for me to move."

"What are you feeling inside right now?"

"Intimidated, afraid, sad, lonely . . . like I want to run and hide."

"Can you imagine looking at them and speaking to them?"

"No. I don't think anything would come out. It would be just like it was in the principal's office. My voice would squeak and they might laugh."

"You're describing some powerful feelings. Where are you putting them all? Your body is rigid and your jaw is fixed."

"I'm keeping them down. I don't want them to see me break. Can we stop now?"

"Yes."

THE NEED TO STAY IN CONTROL

By the time my friend could imagine himself in front of his dad and brother, he was on the brink of exploding. He had a huge well of feelings that were rising like flood waters. The dam that had been built higher year after year was at risk. The pressure was tremendous.

The important thing to realize in what you have just read is that he was completely unaware of the fact that he had unresolved issues with his brother and father. That made it difficult, if not impossible, to completely understand and resolve his crisis at work. As we talked over several weeks' time, the underlying issues became apparent as he unwittingly answered the two questions I asked him at the beginning.

What do you do when you begin to think you're losing control? He stated at the beginning of our conversations that he didn't lose control. I suggested to him that this sounded like a vow. Somewhere inside he said, "I will not let someone see that I need help." He fulfilled that vow by being meticulous and performance oriented, aloof and self-absorbed, suspicious and skeptical.

Flushed Out

When the other teacher went over his head, he felt the threat of being flushed out of his strongholds of self-made safety. He tried to maintain control by several behaviors:

He defended. He believed his ability and integrity were being questioned, and his defensive posture covered his insecurity. Deep inside a voice said, "Someone's finally seen through you. They know you're in trouble."

He rationalized. He analyzed the other teacher's motives, determining the other was threatened by him and afraid his superior teaching ability would usurp his timeworn status. This was another control tactic. As long as he could explain away any possibly justified criticism of the way he was handling his own responsibilities, he could avoid feeling his own fear over an impending loss.

He fantasized. He obsessed about how he would maintain power and control or regain it if the other teacher and principal tried to take it away. By picturing worst-case scenarios, developing a defense against possible exposure, and having an escape, he avoided the reality of feeling little and afraid—not knowing what to do.

The ultimate fantasy in his mind might read: "I'm going to go into that office tomorrow morning and show them all the research I've done. I'm going to dazzle them with piles of paper. If they tell me I'm in over my head and I have to work with someone on the project, I'll submit my resignation and file a grievance with the school board. I'll show them that they picked the wrong person to mess with. I'd better get my résumé out. I might be looking for a new job. I just may need to go someplace where motivation is rewarded."

His sense of control actually returned as soon as the

principal gave him permission to refuse the other teacher's offer of help. When he told me that after he left the principal's office he had a great day, I knew that his regained sense of control told him everything was all right again. In reality, he could not go from having such strong feelings (even to the point of panic and anxiety) to bliss in a matter of seconds. Control was the cap that met his feelings just before they burst, sending them back to the compartment labeled "Do Not Open."

WHAT REALLY HAPPENED?

The second question I asked him to consider held the key to the present: Can you remember losing control at other times in your life?

One time he had lost control and in anger called his brother a name. The consequence left such an impression on him that he could not exercise his voice in any potent anger again. While he could fantasize anger, he couldn't allow it any audible voice.

In addition, he had the feeling of being small—a little person between two giants. Again, his fantasy allowed him to fend for himself. But past reality told him that no one ever stuck up for him. He was on his own, and since he could never break the alliance between his father and brother, he experienced a significant loss. He was extremely verbal when talking to me about the situation, but when trapped between two authority figures, his only viable option was silence. It was the only way to control and hide the panic he felt.

As you can see in this case, rage was not a reaction nearly as much as it was a series of actions aimed at avoiding or preventing what seemed like an intolerable impending loss. It had become a lifestyle of self-protection against threats to control that strip my friend of his dignity.

So then, if rage is a mechanism by which we avoid

powerlessness by maintaining control in potentially over-powering circumstances, over time we learn to rely upon specific control mechanisms that have proven successful in avoiding such loss. We rely on these mechanisms more than we do the grace of God, although only His grace can give real courage and safety. The strongholds of rage in which we feel most secure ultimately resist God's efforts to reach us in crisis.

▼

CHAPTER 7

The Fearful Escape from Truth and Self

IN HER REMARKABLE BOOK, *When Rabbit Howls,* Truddi Chase recalls a childhood that was marked by severe abuse. As a result of her abuse, she developed Multiple Personality Disorder. She explains that she has written the entire book in first person plural because "no one author here [has] total memory of the abuse." The book is the historical account of not one person's memory, but nearly one hundred persons. Listen to her sad commentary on her efforts to resolve loss and ultimately to integrate.

> Added to this [the multiplicity or fragmentation of her personality into many] is the factor of repressed rage. As the rage builds, so does the energy, much like steam in a pressure cooker. . . . Contrary to the established belief that a "well" victim has kissed anger goodbye, we've learned that almost no victim

can completely. Our ending, therefore, is the only
thing in this book that did not really take place,
except as a literary compromise among ourselves.
To the children here who envisioned it, the ending
is quite real, *a comfort created of a rage they will
always hold.*[1] (emphasis mine)

Truddi viewed the possibility of resolution that would
lead to complete integration as impossible. While the nature
of her abuse was extreme and unfamiliar to many of us,
we are not dissimilar in that when we cannot or refuse to
resolve loss, integration of all the parts of us is incomplete.
Integration is necessary for growth and maturity. It
enables us to face increasingly greater losses and take
bigger risks without losing touch with reality through
avoidance mechanisms. If one is not integrating then one
is disintegrating; if not resolving then dissolving.

When you imagine something disintegrating or dissolving, what do you see? The picture is not pretty, is it? So
what holds a disintegrating, dissolving person together?
The answer is rage. Rage creates comfort by convincing
us that without it we cannot survive. We must hold on to
it, but in turn it holds us. The child is no longer without a
parent. Rage has become father and mother, teacher and
counselor, friend and companion.

Rage cannot truly integrate us or bring us to resolution, but it holds us together in an illusion of integration
and resolution by keeping us distant from ourselves and
our truthful responses to loss. In Truddi's case, the distances between parts of herself that experienced loss and
trauma were so great that each part had its own identity
and life apart from the others.

THE ILLUSION OF RESOLUTION AND INTEGRATION

What does it mean to be distant from ourselves? If we are
not like Truddi and haven't suffered the kind or extent of

abuse she has, why should we worry about rage? What if we don't feel separated from ourselves or connected to rage?

Have you ever met someone who seems to have it all together? They work efficiently, talk intelligently, have tremendous social and communication skills, can deal with several things at one time without losing it—you know, the kind of person we all wish we could be?

Martha was that kind of person. She was a secretary for a well-known minister. She had a master's degree in business and was a gifted musician and public communicator. She had a reputation for being someone who reached out to others in need. From every vantage point she appeared to be a mature, functional Christian. That was her public and visible life.

Privately, things were quite different. Martha had a terrible time in her relationships with men. Her most recent relationship with an active alcoholic was abusive. Her boyfriend was a great deal older than she and extremely wealthy. He demanded she be available at his beck and call, but would go weeks without calling her, all the while maintaining relationships with several other women. Martha knew this, but continued to make herself available to him, discounting the degradation and compromise he demanded.

Few people knew of Martha's problem with men. She rarely told the truth about her relationships. Not that she lied to everyone—more accurately, she lied to herself. When she told others how wonderful her boyfriend was, she believed it—or at least wanted to badly enough to ignore the part of her that kept telling her he was not good for her.

She maximized every morsel of attention he gave her and minimized the price she had to pay for those tokens. For her, the price was almost always sex followed by a tirade of criticism about how bad she was in bed. She was then ignored for one to two weeks while his secretary, a "friend of hers," reported to her how many other women he had been seeing since her last call.

How could someone like Martha let herself get involved with such a creep? That's what the group asked her when she told them her story. Martha immediately defended him. She told the group that they just didn't understand him and that she knew him better than anyone else. She then remanded her angry and critical feelings to guilt over having painted a negatively biased picture of a man she wanted everyone to believe was good.

Growing up in an integrational illusion makes living an illusion seem normal. Martha did not grow up in an abusive or unsupportive home. She described her childhood as "normal," and for all purposes, it was. She did grow up, however, with an extremely critical and rigid mother who resented any relationship Martha had with her father. The older Martha got, the more her mother resisted her efforts to engage with her father.

Although her family life appeared "normal" because it didn't contain overt abuse or violence, the disparity between the adult Martha's public and private life was a reflection of the family schism she grew up with but never saw. In other words, under the surface of normalcy was a lot of fear, jealousy, hatred, competition, insecurity—a cesspool of unresolved loss. While it never fully surfaced to create an obvious split in Martha's family, it soiled an increasingly larger percentage of her waking hours as an adult.

Martha did not readily see this problem. In fact, she represented her relationship with her mother as being a close friendship. She spoke of her father as being quiet and to himself, but kind. He was definitely a benevolent background figure. This made it difficult for her to describe specific details of her relationship with him.

To give you an idea of the difference between the way she talked about her mother compared to her dad, here are two small examples.

About Mother

"My mother and I went to the mall yesterday to shop. We spent the entire day together. I was wearing a cute yellow jumper with my hair pulled back in ponytails. It was hot, so I didn't wear close-toed shoes. When my mother saw me, she commented that I looked just like I did when I was little. She then told me I shouldn't have worn blue ribbons in my hair with a yellow jump suit. She told me to take the ribbons out. I did and we left.

"She was in a good mood that day. She talked about her job and all the things she had done that week. She was full of news about the family. We always talk about everyone in the family. Mom must talk to all of our relatives on the phone at least once a week. When I see her on the weekend, she fills me in. She never calls me. She says I'm never home, and anyway, it's my job to call her.

"My relatives must be lonely. They tell my mom everything. She's like their shrink or something. Mom says they talk to her because they know she's a Christian and feel loved by her. I guess they must. I always see cards and letters they send her; she puts them right on the front table. She doesn't let just anyone read them, either. She does let me, though. Last week I read one and made a comment about my aunt who was going through a divorce. Mother got angry at what I said. She told me I shouldn't talk about things I don't know the first thing about. I changed the subject.

"While we were at the mall we went to one of my favorite department stores. I saw a blouse I really liked, but it was out of my price range. My mom was so sweet. She saw how much I wanted it and bought it for me. Oh, that reminds me, I'd better send her a thank-you card. If I don't, she'll remind me what an ungrateful daughter I am and will never forget the time she bought me a blouse and I didn't send a thank-you card. Those cards are really important to her. I guess I understand that since it's certainly the polite thing to do.

We had a really nice day together. I think I'm pretty lucky to have her in my life."

About Dad

"I called my parent's house the other day, looking for my mom, and my dad answered the phone. I was surprised. Usually he's out in the garage or yard doing something. That's his world—he just escapes out there and the rest of us sit and wonder. I can't really remember what we talked about. I think he told me my mother wasn't home and wanted to know if I wanted him to leave a message for her.

"I don't think we talked for more than five minutes. I probably told him what I was doing that evening, and he probably told me that was fine. That's usually what he says. He never gets mad at me. I can't ever remember him yelling or losing his temper. He's just a nice guy who loves his family. I know if I ever needed him, he'd be there for me."

TOXIC WASTE UNDER THE FLOWERS

The Public Martha

In her public life, Martha is a self-sufficient, independent woman who never fails to achieve what she sets out to do. She is extremely task-oriented. The minister she works for is an itinerant teacher, lecturer, and businessman, and her relationship with him entirely revolves around his world. He's not withholding of appreciation or approval for the work she does, but he has very little idea about Martha's personal life, needs, struggles, or pain. He's cordially distant. This is familiar for Martha and much like her relationship with her father. He's bigger than life, but far from hers. A sense of mystery and intrigue surrounds him.

The fact that Martha can work for a great man and feel like his right-hand person is gratifying, and she tells herself she knows things about him that no one else does. Martha is much like her mother in this sense. Knowing the details of someone's life equals importance and intimacy. Reciprocity is not a significant factor. What matters is the need to feel important to someone important.

The only thing in Martha's public life she feels good about is her work. She measures the success of her job by her boss's fame. This feeling of success does not come from something inside herself, but rather from her boss—an external object.

The Private Martha

In her private life, Martha is like a little girl. Her comments about the way she dressed when she went to the mall with her mother are telling, as is the fact that she dates a man significantly older and more successful than she. She not only looks and acts like a little girl, but thinks like one as well. Her public businesswoman image disappears when she steps out of the work arena. Her relationship with her mother and boyfriend are similar in that both:

▼ want to tell her how to think and feel;
▼ want her to be available for them, but do not feel the need to initiate or sustain contact when it doesn't suit their purposes;
▼ punish with criticism and withdrawal;
▼ reward in a way that makes them her benefactors and therefore indebted to them;
▼ demand loyalty, but feel no responsibility for mutual respect.

The obvious difference between the two is how they accomplish their agendas. Her boyfriend is overtly abusive and punishing. Her mother, on the other hand, is very subtle. She would, in fact, be critical of Martha's boyfriend if she knew how he treated her. Neverthe-less, the effect of each person's treatment is the same. Martha is unable to be honest enough about her losses and respect herself enough to feel the degradation, humiliation, and belittlement she experiences in each relationship.

THE NATURE OF SEPARATION

While Martha said a lot about her day with her mother, she also left out a great deal. I began by saying that rage separates us from ourselves. Martha functions like two different people because the part of her that knows the truth cannot communicate with the part of her that is controlled by lies.

For example, if someone came into the group and told Martha's story in her presence, she would be the first one to ask why the person is allowing herself to be treated so badly. She would then recommend books, tapes, seminars, and other helping tools, saying, "I've read some really good things about what you're going through that I think will help." She would likely say all of that, yet be completely blind to the fact that the other person is telling her story.

Martha is more integrated in her public world. She is able to reason and make good choices because she has to—it is expected and required. She is also rewarded for it by her position and responsibility. Her boss doesn't need a little girl who can't tell up from down. He needs a capable, responsible adult who can run the ship when he's gone. Martha steps in and functions flawlessly. If someone were to challenge her work, decisions, or authority, she would be able to communicate her own feelings and negotiate until a mutual understanding was reached.

Since Martha was a capable decisionmaker in her public world, she had to ignore all the internal messages in her private world that told her she was capable and didn't need to be treated like a child. The part of her that learned to relate to her mother, and later to her boyfriend, like a little girl had long since suppressed any part of her personality that either one of them might view as threatening, demanding, or adult.

INTERNAL EDITING

As I previously mentioned, Martha left a great deal out of her detailed report of the day at the mall with Mom. She tended to report the same way when talking about her weekends with her boyfriend. She was careful to include details about her mother's and boyfriend's lives and what they did together. But she left herself out—her feelings, views, reactions, needs, observations, and opinions.

She didn't consciously leave out these details, she simply told the story the way she remembered it. More accurately, she told the story the way she wanted and needed to remember it. An editing process was in full speed while she was at the mall. By the time she got to our group, she had completely removed all of the scenes that would have shown her true relationship with her mother.

For Martha to see the truth, she had to have someone walk her through her story to help her hear the truthful voice that she edited. She had to be willing to listen to her pain about the reality of her relationship with her mother compared to the ideal picture she painted for herself and others.

The wonderful day at the mall that Martha portrayed was actually a terrible day that left Martha angry and depressed for the rest of that evening. Since she couldn't connect that anger and depression with her time with her mother, she blamed it on the fact that her boyfriend had not called her. She came home to a silent answering machine.

COMPARTMENTS OF DENIAL

Integration and resolution cannot occur without a commitment to looking honestly at our relationships and how they do or do not meet up to our expectations and ideals. Martha had separated herself from her disappointment and anger so that her pictures of her relationships with people she loved were distorted and unrealistic.

Since she couldn't actually achieve integrity and resolution through real confrontation, she turned to an illusion of integrity and resolution. At that point, rage comes into the picture. By creating separations or compartments in which she locked her unacceptable feelings and perceptions, she was able to function as though she had intimate and nurturing relationships, when in fact she was desperate for more.

The degree of unresolved loss a person has, as well as the age(s) during which the loss(es) took place, have some bearing on when he or she first begins to separate various parts of himself or herself from the whole and on how deep those separations are. Someone like Truddi Chase, whose first significant trauma occurred at age two, has very deep separations to the point of developing multiple personalities.

Most of us have separation, but not to the point that we have parts of us that are unaware of what other parts of us are doing. Martha could sense her anger, discontentment, and unhappiness in her relationship with her mother. She could not, however, allow those feelings to compete with her need to prove her loyalty. In her mind, she had to be completely loyal, which meant she could not complain or be unhappy. People who separate from their authentic feelings in this way usually view things in black-and-white terms.

We are all broken and distant from ourselves to some extent. When we drop a glass, how it breaks depends on how far it fell, what it hit at the bottom, and where it landed. We all have been dropped in this life and are therefore broken to some degree.

Some of us are broken, but still intact. We have a lot of cracks and are fragile. We can't contain or tolerate anything that might stress our weaknesses and therefore break us further. To protect ourselves, we make rules and laws about how we should be touched, handled, and used. As long as those rules and laws are followed, we feel safe and even forget that we are cracked.

I don't want to be fragile!

Others of us are broken in pieces, strewn across the floor. With a little glue and time, we can be put back together, almost as good as new. We have some of the same laws and rules as the others because we too are fragile.

Finally, some of us are so broken and our pieces are so dispersed that we feel like the proverbial Humpty Dumpty. Try as we may, we cannot see how we will ever be put back together again.

Wherever this book finds you, we all have one thing in common—we are broken. Whether cracked or shattered, we cannot truly fix ourselves. The thought that we can is an illusion. We are helpless to do anything. The better we understand that truth, the more rage loses its grip upon us.

Am I really a strong person or is it an illusion?

Rage wants to keep us believing that no one knows how to care for us better than we do. It exalts and applauds self-reliance. It taunts, "Where was your God when you were being broken . . . and where is He now? Not even He can help you." It warns us not to trust Him. It even says, "If you do trust Him, He will only fix you to break you again. What kind of cruel thing is that?"

To be whole people, we cannot allow rage to be the integrating and resolving force in our lives. Its attempts at both involve deception, manipulation, and extortion. As long as we allow rage to tell us what to do, we will only keep adding unresolved loss onto our existing pile of unresolved loss. The person who carries rage through life eventually disintegrates and dissolves, not integrates and resolves. Rage manifests itself in broken marriages, estrangement from children, isolation, bitterness, hopelessness, and cynicism.

What begins as a comfort, ends as what Solomon so appropriately refers to as "meaningless." Unhealed and untouched by God's grace, we resign ourselves to hopeless existence.

▼

CHAPTER 8

The Ruthless Defense
Against Conflict

I REMEMBER SINGING a repetitive yet insightful song as a six-year-old that goes something like this:

> There was an old lady who swallowed a fly,
> I don't know why she swallowed a fly,
> Perhaps she'll die . . .

The song goes on to record the various "critters" she ingested in her efforts to remove the fly. She swallowed a spider to catch the fly, a bird to catch the spider, a cat to catch the bird, a dog to catch the cat, a cow to catch the dog, and finally—a horse. The final words of the song tell us her fate:

> There was an old lady who swallowed a horse,
> She's dead, of course.

How do we go from swallowing flies to horses and

that's in between? In chapters 5 and 6, I talked about how we use control and performance to step around, over, under, or away from loss, thus creating a false sense of safety. In chapter 7, I added the concept of distancing from ourselves by sealing off truckloads of unresolved loss in inner "compartments," thus dulling our soul to truth. Controlling, performing, and distancing from our own truth are all mechanisms of rage. They keep us free of the quicksand of loss and grief that we're certain will suck us under if we get too close.

In this chapter, I want to add another group of mechanisms to rage's avoidance portfolio. Defense mechanisms often are employed when conflict threatens to strip us of our self-protective control. While the mechanisms discussed in previous chapters often operate at an unconscious level, we consciously choose defense mechanisms to protect against the imminent exposure of the hidden shame and helplessness associated with loss.

With each unresolved loss, a certain degree of self-blame and shame over having been victimized takes form. Loss has a way of reminding us that we are human and vulnerable, and at some level we believe it is wrong to be either. To carry the label "victim" means that somehow we have been disqualified from the world of "normal" people who seem to live on the better side of life's tracks.

A defense mechanism sweeps loss and the associated shame and helplessness under the carpet. It restores an appearance of normalcy and offers others the security of knowing they are not in a relationship with a loser.

If I could rewrite the song about the Old Lady and her "critters" to illustrate the woman's thought process while she was ingesting all of those bugs and animals, it might sound something like this: Oops, I swallowed a fly. How could I have done that? I wasn't paying attention. If I had kept my mouth closed instead of talking so much, I wouldn't have swallowed it. What am I going to do? I should call the doctor, but I can't do that. The last time I swallowed a fly and went to the doctor, my husband went through the roof. He took one look at the bill and told me if I swallowed any more flies I would just have to live with it—even if it killed me. He thinks I did it on purpose for attention. Why would I do something like that? I can't convince him, though.

Let's pause for a minute to look at the issues with which she's dealing. Something bad happened—she swallowed a fly. To make things worse, this is the second one she's swallowed, and her husband had fits over the first one because getting it out cost a lot of money. Can you hear her shame, helplessness, and the responsibility she carries for having done that? Somehow it's all her fault— both swallowing the fly and her husband's anger. In comes the first defense mechanism to sweep the event under the carpet.

> I can't let anyone know I have swallowed this
> fly . . . but I can't stand having it buzz around
> inside of me. What will I do? I know, spiders eat
> flies; I'll find one and swallow that.

The rest of the story is history. She swallows bigger bugs and animals until what she swallowed was bigger than her holding capacity. She killed herself with her defensive cures.

As I previously mentioned, we consciously choose defense mechanisms. This doesn't mean we always know why we do what we do, nor does it suggest that the defenses we choose are logical or sensible. Having our actions make sense is often less important than getting rid of the bothersome buzz that reminds us we are victims. Let me use the Old Lady one more time to illustrate this point.

Upon swallowing a fly, she finds herself in the company of her many Christian friends who have never swallowed flies and can't possibly relate to people who do. At a prayer meeting, our Old Lady is beside herself because she fears her friends will hear the fly buzzing around inside her and discover, to her shame, that she is one of the "poor unfortunates" who swallowed a fly. Disgusted by the idea of becoming the object of someone's pity and terrified of the labels associated with being helpless, the Old Lady explains that she must go home to take care of an important matter that she'd completely forgotten until now. Refusing offers for rides, assistance, and advice, she leaves with her fly buzzing and sighs with relief over having escaped unexposed.

Me at Church

To the objective observer, it makes no sense for the woman to hide her dilemma. What better place to get help than from a group of prayerful and supportive friends? Options and choices are always easier to explore, however, when we are not faced with immediate exposure. Defense mechanisms have one important priority: *Get me out of here quickly before someone sees me!*

DEFENSIVE AVOIDANCE

Perhaps the most fertile ground in which rage takes root as defensive avoidance is in potential or actual relational conflict with the significant people in our lives. Early in childhood, we learn how to employ various defense mechanisms to willfully and consciously protect ourselves from events and people that might expose our shame.

Our conscious defense resolutions are rooted in unconscious needs to avoid. Needless to say, defensive postures keep us from legitimately resolving our losses because these postures will not allow us to expose our helplessness to God or others.

Rage-rooted distortions about loss and truth inevitably make a mess of our relationships. Always seeking to prevent loss by maintaining self-protective control, we block out God's grace and truth that could keep us from relational deception and destruction. The most common relational distortions that people struggle with today are codependency and addiction.

CODEPENDENCY AND ADDICTION

Our most basic struggles in our current relationships revolve around our attempts to get our needs met or to meet others' need. Unresolved loss makes it impossible to put our past to rest. Where there is loss, there is a need. To effectively resolve conflict, we must accurately identify and meet our needs. To do so, we must listen to ourselves and validate our needs as legitimate. We must then listen to others and accept their stated or implied limits for meeting our needs. And we must listen to God and accept His offer to be our Father and heal our wounds.

Codependency is a symptom of unresolved loss. It is another of rage's mechanisms for avoiding reality by distorting one's view of self and others. Codependency is an "omnipotent" view of oneself in relationship with a perceived "impotent" other.

Because the word *codependency* has been so overused, let me offer my definition. Codependency is a threefold distortion of how God intended human relationships to function. It is the means by which we:

▼ cover over our terminal neediness by endless performance;
▼ fearfully resist healthy intimacy and autonomy;
▼ hide our efforts to be worshiped and adored behind a veil of "caring" for others' needs.

Performance perpetuates the lie that acceptance is dependent upon meritorious effort and is the only path to needed gratification. Focusing on and trying to meet another's needs puts us in a "meaningful" relationship while we remain hidden and untouched in our "safe" isolation. When the other-centered performance does not illicit worship and adoration—well, you know where that goes.

The mirror image of codependency is addiction. It is another avoidance mechanism of rage. It is a fabricated state of acceptability achieved through self-fulfillment and self-gratification, an attempt to abort oneself from dependence on someone else's conditional nurture.

The co-dependency/addiction cycle in relationships is a common human resource for conflict resolution. Since both resolve conflict by avoiding it, no true closure on either end takes place and, therefore, no fulfillment of need takes place either. Parties on both sides end up emaciated with need, and without truthful intervention, emotional death by starvation is a certainty.

DEFENSE IN ACTION

Guilt
In all relationships in which avoidance of conflict and loss is a priority, specific defense mechanisms become active and reliable. Guilt is a telltale symptom of active defensive mechanisms rooted in rageful avoidance. When a cloud of guilt over your head rains "I should" or "I ought to have" statements upon you, you are likely living with a proportionate amount of hidden shame rooted in unresolved loss.

Guilt, however unpleasant, assures us our defense mechanisms are working. We would rather feel guilty than defenseless. Guilt is the ransom we are willing to pay to keep our losses secret.

The exchange of shame for guilt is our way of bringing public exposure and helplessness into a private domain wherein we have some sense of control. I have not found a better description of this exchange than the one in *Too Scared to Cry*, a book by renowned child psychiatrist Dr. Lenore Terr:

As a protection against feeling ashamed . . . young
people make delayed, unconscious trade-offs—
"guilt" for "shame." . . . Shame comes from public
exposure of one's own vulnerability. Guilt on the
other hand, is private. It follows from a sense of
failing to measure up to private, internal standards.
When others "know" that you once were helpless,
you tend to feel ashamed. THEY know. If, on the
other hand, you feel you caused your own problems,
you cease feeling so vulnerable and blame yourself,
instead, for the shape of events. YOU know. But you
are the only one.[1]

Defense mechanisms are like escape hatches—they
are doors marked "Emergency Exit" when conflict in relationships starts to get too difficult or threatening. Below, I
have identified four such "exits." Perhaps you will find the
hinges on these doors to be well-worn in your own life.

Lying

I found myself sitting across from a young man who stated
rather matter-of-factly, "I'm a chronic liar." I must have
looked surprised because he then added, "At least that's
what everyone tells me." I told him that most of the
chronic liars I knew weren't so honest. I asked him to
tell me why he felt the need to lie, and he spent nearly
an hour explaining how difficult it was to please all the
people in his world. "You're damned if you do and damned
if you don't," he said. "It's easier just to tell people what
they want to hear."

"How do you feel about lying?" I asked.

"Guilty," he admitted. "I don't like to do it. My parents
and girlfriend say they can't trust me anymore. I just try
not to get caught."

"What happens when you do?"

"I just take my punishment, what else can I do?"

I finished our conversation by saying, "You're not a

pathological liar. You lie because you feel trapped—it seems like the only way to keep everyone happy. Your problem isn't lying; it's fear of how you think others will treat you when you fail to please them. Lying is your way of controlling your world. As long as you can lie, you don't have to face reality. Lies are perfect escapes."

People pleasers are among the most sincere liars I know. Lying is the defensive exit they use when they feel they are going to be confronted for having failed to meet someone's expectations. They are the individuals who tell "little white lies" and who rationalize them by telling themselves, "It won't hurt anyone. Besides, people would understand if they were in my shoes."

Our lady who swallowed the fly was definitely a people pleaser. She told several white lies when she thought her problem was going to incite conflict or ruin someone else's good time. But lying as a defense mechanism leads us to forms of problem solving that can wound or kill us.

We must listen to our own white lies and ask ourselves, "How am I using this to protect myself from exposure, and what do I fear will happen if I tell the truth?" Chances are we'll discover the dread of shameful exposure as foolish or inadequate—worthy of rejection. Guilt over lying is the easier route.

Arguing

Not all arguing is part of defensive avoidance. Argument as defense against exposure involves the need to be right or have the last word. All of us know people who will defend themselves to their dying breath with one excuse after another.

Unable to accept responsibility for what is truly theirs (and the shameful exposure that goes along with it), they surround us with a whirlwind of rationalization and dizzying explanation. The genius of this kind of defense is that it usually contains a measure of truth that makes the confronter feel uncertain, too harsh, unreasonable, and over time, downright exasperated.

People who defend themselves through argument are trying to forestall exposure that might lead to rejection or harsh treatment. As long as they can keep their accuser engaged in trying to prove (fruitlessly) that his gripe is legitimate, there is no resolution and therefore no final judgment. Mission accomplished!

If this defense mechanism is one of your favorites, try asking yourself why you are so dedicated to proving your innocence. Feel guilty? Maybe you'll be able to think back to a time in your life when someone did not believe you. How was the truth you told rejected or discounted? What was the consequence? Did you feel ashamed? Chances are you've learned how to dodge the shame of being discredited by vehemently denying any guilt you ever feel.

Acquiescence

This exit might be called the art of giving in. The person who uses it defends by not defending. I spoke with a frustrated wife who complained that her husband wouldn't engage in any conflict. "It doesn't matter what I want to discuss, he just says he doesn't want to fight about it and that I should do whatever I want to do." Her primary frustration was feeling alone and completely responsible for everything.

In talking to men like this woman's husband, I have found that most of them can remember choosing this strategy as a way of avoiding conflict and the potentially devastating consequence of shameful exposure. One man said, "I was tired of hearing her complain about everything. She thought she could do things better, so I decided to let her. I just let her do what she wants to do. Maybe she'll see that things aren't so easy."

Can you hear the anger and passive aggressive control in those words? People who use the strategy of protection and control through silence actually have plenty to say, but rather than being honest and risking conflict, they stand back and wait for the right opportunity to emerge triumphant.

It would be wrong to conclude that individuals who choose this kind of defense are malicious—or at least more so than those choosing other defensive escapes. While their behavior may be motivated partly by needs for vindication, their objective is primarily to stay safe. Acquiescence is born from feelings of inadequacy, exasperation, and hopelessness. For people whose safety net is rage instead of God, it becomes the only way out when talking or arguing lead to the threat of entrapment or loss of dignity through criticism.

Mud-Slinging

I recently overheard this conversation between two men, "I have just enough psychological training to be dangerous. When my wife comes to confront me, I know enough about her issues to throw the whole problem back on her."

Mud-slinging is a combination of blame-shifting and score-keeping. Expert mud-slingers avoid exposure by exposing the person confronting them as being at least as bad, if not worse. While heading for the exit, mud-slingers seem to have rapid-fire recall regarding everything their partner has done in the past hundred years. They are remarkably successful at throwing their "enemy" off balance.

TEARING DOWN THE WALLS

Recognizing our escapes, as benign as they may seem, is an important step toward uncovering the rage-partitions that keep us from connecting with our loss and healthy emotion. As long as we cling to these defense mechanisms, we will not resolve our losses and will therefore keep others at arm's length.

Tearing down the defensive walls that have served to

protect us for many years is tough—especially when we feel our "loved ones" are still keeping theirs firmly intact. Much like the Cold War of the last two decades, each side is waiting for the other to lay down arms before a treaty is signed.

While it takes time to locate and dismantle the walls, it is a task well worth undertaking. Accepting responsibility for what we are consciously aware of gives God the freedom to work in our subconscious to restructure and prepare our hearts to bear the burden of legitimate suffering associated with grief and the relinquishment of rage.

In the next section we will turn to the steps we need to take to undress our rage and posture ourselves to be clothed in the mercy of God.

PART THREE

▼

RESOLUTION:
How Can We Relinquish Our Rage?

▼

CHAPTER 9

Confrontation: Allowing Truth to Penetrate Our Defenses

RAGE CANNOT BE ELIMINATED until we allow the truth to penetrate its defenses. Rage is much like a general mounted behind troops. His purpose is to make sure the war-torn person continues to run from truth and therefore never resolves loss. Resolution of loss cannot occur without an invitation for the truth to shine in every corner (known and hidden) of our beings. Once activated, the truth leads us to the discovery of the rage that has kept us from deeply honest and meaningful relationships with ourselves, others, and God.

We all have different degrees of resistance to letting the truth work. The truth is like a sword—it cuts, divides, and separates. That sounds painful, and it is. Since our history of exposure is largely connected to public shame and helplessness, the idea of giving ourselves over to exposure again, especially to God's penetrating eye, is difficult to embrace. But if we really want to defeat rage's rule in our lives, we must be willing to confront our commitments to defensive pride, denial, self-nurture, and self-concealment.

CONFRONTING DEFENSIVE PRIDE

Opening the door to truth begins with confronting the strongholds we maintain apart from God. Pride protects us from discovering and admitting that we need help and can't change without it. It is determined to be anti-dependent and omnipotent—a power unto itself.

We are all prideful in that we are fallen, sinful creatures. But the particular kind of defensive pride I'm referring to is rooted in unresolved loss. Remember, the rage walls we build are set on a foundation of determined self-reliance by which we deny our deepest needs for God's grace and upon the attempt to save ourselves by providing for our needs.

Rage Versus Outrage

To illustrate why we become proud instead of humbly dependent, we must compare rage and outrage. In telling a story about her granddaughter, a woman began, "I think we need some kind of rage to survive." She went on to say that she was watching her granddaughter play with some older boys. As is typically true, the boys didn't want a little girl bothering them. Her every effort to join was met with resistance until she exploded with frustration, anger, and hurt.

"I could see the rage in this small child," the grandmother said. "I think it was necessary. What was happening to her was unfair, and she reacted honestly. If she didn't have the ability to feel outrage over injustice, she may have had no means for self-protection, in that situation or in the future."

Anytime something is taken from us, our normal and healthy response is to be outraged. It is that part of us

that senses injustice and demands restoration. Ou
is our resistance to the evil that can produce or perpe-
trate loss. Outrage drives us to find a protector outside
of ourselves. When the woman's granddaughter could not
negotiate a fair settlement with the boys she wanted to
play with, she ran to her grandmother for support. Support in this case would mean comfort, protection, listening, understanding, and intervention on some level. That
kind of support helps bring resolution because the injustice and resulting outrage are not internalized and transformed into defensive rage walls against the world.

What happens if we turn to a protector in our outrage
and find none? What would have happened if the little girl
turned to her grandmother only to hear criticism, anger,
blame, or disinterest? She would have no one to validate
the injustice she suffered and therefore would have no
ability to resolve the loss she felt when the boys wouldn't
let her play with them.

This lack of a protector paves the way for rage to
develop. Rooted in unresolved loss and covered over with
omnipotent pride, these situations make people who cannot or will not look outside themselves for support their
own sole and soul supporter. This means that instead
of reaching out for comfort, protection, and help, they
reach inside themselves, relying upon their own abilities
to solve problems and right wrongs.

Rage functions on a basic belief that there isn't anyone out there to hear our pain or see our injustice. Added
to that may be the experience of having our pain and
injustice mocked or shamed by statements such as the
following:

▼ "Stop crying or I'll give you something to cry
about."
▼ "Stop being such a baby! Get out there and
defend yourself."
▼ "Don't come to me, I'm sure you did something to

start it."

▼ "Stop bothering them. Just leave them alone and then they won't tease you."

While statements like these may have been intended to help or toughen us for our own good, they have made us self-reliant and internally dependent for protecting and maintaining ourselves in the face of loss or injustice. Said another way, we have learned to take the law into our own hands and exact punishment on those who break it according to what our rage dictates.

An Example
Take for example a mother who loses a child. Such a loss is an unacceptable loss. It doesn't fit with her ideals. In her outrage, she might say, "Why did this happen to me?" or "What did I do to deserve this?"

What if this mother had grown up believing that when she lost something she loved, it was her fault? What if the protectors in her life responded to her outrage by telling her she deserved to lose something she cared about because she was irresponsible? How is she going to answer her own questions about the loss of her child? How will she reach out and what kind of support will she look for? What will she say to the person who tells her it wasn't her fault? Won't some part of her believe it was?

She will likely conclude that the loss would not have happened had she not been bad. Her failure to be responsible becomes the reason for bad happenings. Her internal rage (the illegitimate mechanism by which she can steer clear of the depth of her legitimate grief and loneliness) would demand that she figure out what she did wrong.

She must then vow never to be bad again and find a punishment suitable to her crime. She may conclude (consciously or subconsciously) that she can never have another baby. Justice is executed and she becomes infertile. Sound unbelievable? You'd be amazed at the power of our rage to control even our biological choices.

The important thing to realize is that the mother who lost her child resolved the loss completely within herself. Her inability to reach out for support was rooted, at least in part, in a belief that the unfair things in life were somehow her own doing—as if she were all-powerful. Can you hear a voice out of her past saying, "Don't come to me. I don't feel a bit sorry for you. I told you not to let that puppy go out of the yard. Maybe now you'll learn to take better care of things."

We are not all-powerful nor are we capable of taking care of our deepest needs without intervention. We are in desperate need of healing from a source outside ourselves. If only we could recognize and relinquish our rageful pride so that we might turn to the Living God and find the power of His presence and mercy that gives dignity to our deepest losses.

CONFRONTING DENIAL

Denial is not purposeful dishonesty, although people in denial can be dishonest. The expression, "She looks at the world through rose-colored glasses," refers to someone who is missing something—filtering reality so as to see only what she wants to see.

Some people use denial to filter anything that might be termed bad or negative. Others filter anything that might be termed good or positive. Denial is the basic mechanism we use to color our world so the picture won't change and throw us off balance.

Ultimately, denial is a form of control. It helps us feel safe when we can't overcome or resolve loss. The greater the loss and the more helpless we are to resolve it, the more powerful the denial will be. When someone's denial gets to the point that they can no longer distinguish between reality and fantasy, they are considered mentally ill and are difficult to help.

When we deny loss, we deny its impact on us and our resulting need. If we cannot see ourselves as having needs, then we really have no reason to reach out for help. Since God presents Himself as a Savior to help us in our calamity, we are by virtue of our denial at odds with Him in that role. To accept Him as such would mean to have our perception of ourselves and our world altered—to have our rose-colored glasses removed.

We all come into relationship with God wearing rose-colored glasses. His purpose from the beginning has been to help us see how we deny reality and then bring us to a point of willingness to have our concepts restructured or changed. This can be a painful process since it can change the way we see our loved ones, ourselves, our heroes, and our villains. Denial functions to protect us from such disillusionment.

Disillusionment

Disillusionment, or the breaking down of denial, occurs in three stages. First, we discover our illusions about life.

Second, we accept that our fantasies may never materialize.

Third, we allow truth to replace illusion.

Progress through these stages can take a long time. Naturally, the more unresolved loss a person carries, the more illusions he or she has about life. Specific illusions reflect the kinds of unresolved losses carried. In other words, if a person's unresolved loss is rooted in a power issue, then his or her illusions will revolve around power.

A good example of this is a man who came to a group to deal with his struggle with homosexuality. Jason's mother left him and his father when Jason was five. He never saw her again. He lost his father to cancer when he was eight and was then raised by his relationally distant and enigmatic paternal grandparents. Jason remembered watching his father rapidly decline with his illness. Within a year of diagnosis, he was dead. Jason remembered feeling powerless to help him and terrified of losing him. He didn't fully understand cancer, but knew people could and often did die from it. Now twenty-seven years old, he struggles with an inability to feel whole in his masculinity.

A recurring illusion of heroism filled Jason's sexual relationships and fantasies. Both his real and fantasized sexual relationships were with men who were usually much older than he and in need of care. He fantasized about being a strong, loving, and paternal presence who would ultimately have the power to heal or restore the object of his fantasy. He would then imagine himself having the perfect relationship—one in which he could share his most intimate feelings and be understood.

The power of this illusion cannot be understated. It took more than a year for Jason to recognize the theme to his sexual fantasies and exploits. Jason's losses were many. One of his greatest losses was that of power. Unable to fix his dad, he watched him die. It's no wonder that one of Jason's strongest illusions revolved around a power theme—one in which he could save someone and make life perfect.

How did Jason begin to enter into the stages of disillusionment? Not quickly or easily. The discovery of the illusions that drove him in relationships did not immediately solve his problems with men or take away his desire to be with them. It did, however, help him turn a significant corner as he realized that as long as he continued to try to save someone, he would deny the real pain of losing his father and his own powerlessness over helplessly watching him die.

The second stage of disillusionment was much more painfully difficult. Jason could never get his dad back. As long as he held onto his illusion, he never had to fully admit or feel that agonizing truth. Letting go of the fantasy would mean fully embracing the loss of his father. That would mean feeling eight years old again, powerless, terrified, and grief-stricken. For Jason, the thought of going back to face the loss felt like death. It took another six months before he found the courage to let go of his illusions and embrace the painful truth.

Once sufficiently disillusioned, we are faced with our own need and helplessness. At this point, the rage-driven mechanisms of self-nurture and self-concealment work to convince us that we must keep our needs and helplessness to ourselves. They keep us from reaching out, or when we do, they set the parameters for what we will and won't accept in terms of intervention.

CONFRONTING SELF-NURTURE

Self-nurture is healthy in the fact that we must learn to recognize and care for our needs. This does not mean, however, that we don't depend upon others for a variety of assistance and support. People who are too dependent won't recognize and care for their own needs for autonomy. People who are too independent won't recognize and care for their needs for intimacy or community. People striving for interdependence will know when they need community and when they need solitude. This knowledge is the essence of appropriate self-nurture.

Rage-driven self-nurture occurs when we go underground with our needs, taking them into the caverns of our own souls. This automatically creates a secret world in which we maintain ourselves with little or no thought of reaching out for assistance.

When Jason lost his father, he lost his sense of safety as well as power. Because those losses were never resolved (he never fully grieved his father's death in a supportive community), his needs went largely unnoticed and unmet. Since no one existed in his world to respond to his need when his father died, he wasn't able to reach out for the nurturing he needed. He learned to take his dependency needs inside himself and to manage them so that later in life he didn't appear to be insecure or bereaved.

What feeds us in that secret cavern where we hide in our pain? Can we really take care of ourselves in that way? The answer is no. Over time, the deprivation (physical, emotional, spiritual) forces us out of hiding, at which point we are compelled to meet our needs. However, many of us can't identify our deepest needs. As a result, it's easy to look to illegitimate sources to get them met. If we find some comfort in the illegitimate source, we take it gladly over the alternative, which is nothing.

It took Jason a long time to realize he needed to feel safe and powerful. He thought he needed intimacy and sex with other men. Confronting Jason meant helping him see the illegitimacy in his own self-nurture and giving him opportunity to risk reaching out from the hidden part of him for the help he needed when he was a young boy.

CONFRONTING SELF-CONCEALMENT

Self-concealment began thousands of years ago when Adam bought a lie and exposed himself to shame. The fact that he hid himself from God because of his shame makes it clear that when we buy lies, they will drive us into hiding every time.

When we experience loss, we are in need of truthful intervention. When it is not forthcoming, we internalize the loss and, at some level, hold ourselves responsible for having caused it. This human tendency is compounded when those around us heap blame or guilt upon our already wounded hearts. We come to interpret loss through the grid of other people's rage. When that happens, we ingest countless distortional lies that urge us to conceal ourselves or else die.

Jason's self-concealment was reflected in his adult lifestyle. He truly believed he was trapped in homosexuality

and defended its legitimacy on the basis of his inability
to change. In his deepest parts, he did not believe anyone, even God, could help him. His heroism functioned to
resist help because it needed to do the rescuing. On a less
conscious level, Jason's self-concealment was wrapped up
in his unresolved loss of power and his contempt for his
own weakness.

I've already suggested that Jason was beginning to
see aspects of his pride, denial, self-nurture, and self-
concealment and that those discoveries were a long time
in coming. What happened to his sexual behavior? Did he
stop struggling sexually? As he allowed God to undress
his rage, did he change?

It's natural for us to want to see hope and expect permanent change. Jason's growth away from his heroism
(which was the driving force behind his sexual issues) is
still in progress. He still struggles with his sexuality and
his needs for male involvement. He is, however, accepting
his brokenness and shedding the garment of heroism. It's
tough. He cries a lot and feels angry. He is often mad at
God, and sometimes at me. He doesn't like to hear me say
that he has a disabling wound, that he must stop taking
care of others and start attending to his own damage and
sin. Sometimes he listens, and other times he does what
rage dictates.

In the final analysis, Jason is changing. He is allowing God to strip off his garment of rage one fiber at a time.
He's worn it for so long that it feels like part of him, and
sometimes he doesn't think he'll survive the stripping
process. But with each new layer of rage that falls to
the ground, Jason has been met with liberating truth
and cleansing mercy. Sometimes he sees it immediately;
freedom seems real and hope unconquerable. It doesn't
always happen this way, but he's more accepting of the
process and understands that there are times when the
struggle will feel as strong and overpowering as it did in
the beginning.

MEETING JESUS IN OUR PAIN

As Christians, we struggle with the human question, "How can Jesus allow us to be subjected to abuse if He knows that it creates the potential for rage and teaches us to avoid loss?"

The answer isn't easy, but that doesn't mean we shouldn't attempt to answer it. Jesus acknowledged our vulnerability to abuse. He also lived in an abusive world and was subject to abuse at the hands of calculating and powerful perpetrators who eventually succeeded in killing Him. What He suffered was anything but fair by anyone's standards.

Not only was He the victim, but so were those who looked on helplessly while a corrupt, evil, and prejudicial system had Him beaten, stripped, and paraded through the streets. I'm certain that the memory of those last hours never left the minds of those who lived with Him, loved Him, and were loved by Him.

While this book is not specifically about abuse, we must understand how it produces loss and encourages us to build rage walls of protection. While some forms of abuse are more insidious than others, in all of its forms it is destructive, unjust, and incomprehensible. When we are wounded by it, we need to believe that Someone who knows our suffering is able to help us navigate through the deep waters of unanswerable questions, inconsolable grief, and unquenchable outrage to restoration's shore.

If you cannot comprehend that Jesus is your partner in suffering by virtue of His own agony and loss, you have not yet experienced the most mysterious part of His deity—His humanity. A stained-glass Jesus will bring you no comfort or solace unless you abandon reality and join Him high above the pain and suffering in pious suspension.

The deepest question should not be why He allows us to suffer loss at the hands of perpetrating others, but why

He promises to help us endure the suffering by ensuring His presence in the midst of it. For victims of abuse, this question is both incredible and outrageous. The record of their own abuse plays back scene after scene of suffering, revealing no one there to cut through the abandonment, pain, confusion, betrayal, and shock.

For these victims, the stained-glass Jesus seems more substantive than the human one. The idea that there could be any outrage, passion, or agony expressed on their behalf over the injustices suffered from a source outside themselves is difficult to grasp and hold on to. To believe that their own expressions of outrage, passion, or agony in response to the pain and suffering matter and are heard by One who has promised to bring comfort and ultimate justice to the wrongs we have suffered is even more difficult.

It always has been, and continues to be, God's job to enlarge our concepts to see beyond what our wounded eyes will allow. I recently had my own vision enlarged in a powerful and life-changing way. For reasons unknown to me, God often talks to me when I'm swimming in the pool. It's probably the only time He can get in a word.

An Inside Look
One day as I was swimming, a headline caption floated across my mind in bold letters: "THE DAY JESUS CAME HOME."

I then saw a scene between a father and his son that struck me to the core. The son walked through the door of what looked like his home. I knew that he'd accomplished a great feat and endured great pain. I also knew that he was victorious. His first expression, however, was not one of triumph. He didn't seem eager to go to the welcome-home party and tell everyone what had happened.

He stood for a moment in front of his father. They made eye contact and neither spoke for what seemed like a long time. It was as if they were conversing visually—

almost as though the son's eyes were playing back the scenes of his suffering for his father's eyes to absorb. It seemed as though his father's eyes reassured his son that there was no part of what he was viewing that had gone unnoticed, unfelt, or unrecorded.

I saw the son's eyes pool with tears. The father's eyes remained fixed on him. After the silence, the son broke in with words so deep with feeling it is hard for me to describe the sound of them. He looked at his father and said, "That was the hardest thing I've ever done. It was so painful . . . I never knew how difficult that would be."

His tears fell hard and seemed to mean relief more than triumph. The weight finally removed and the ordeal behind him, he could let himself feel small again—in need of comfort, embrace, empathy, and warmth.

The father responded with more than understanding. It was as though he had been through the ordeal as well. He answered, "That was the hardest thing I've ever done. To watch you in agony. The hardest part for me was to see you cry out for me and not be able to hear me say 'I'm here! I haven't gone anywhere.' The outrage I had over what I saw happening to you . . . It took all I had not to destroy them all."

They embraced for a long time—laughed, cried, sang, sat in silence, and did it all over again until each had fully exchanged the experience.

You might wonder if I am prone to hallucinations. No, I just think God met me with a vivid picture of Himself that I needed to see that day in the pool. I am still attempting to absorb all of what that picture meant. Immediately and simply, it helped me visualize the manner in which Jesus shares and participates in our suffering. I believe we need such images in order to believe that the pictures of our own abuse are not lost or forgotten by One who loved us enough to call us out of its destructive cycle.

Many people experience abuse in childhood before they have any deep understanding or experience of God's outrage over an evil world, His compassion for the weak and victimized, and His ultimate plan to heal all wounds and right all wrongs in a coming Kingdom. Therefore, most of us learn early to build rage walls that temporarily and superficially protect us from a sense of helplessness in a frightening world. As terrifying as it is at first to tear down those walls, it is the only way into our Father's arms.

It is the hiding of ourselves and our shame from God that keeps us captive to the lies that got us there. We will forever fear God in our hiding until we risk stepping out in our nakedness to discover that He has known all along how shameful we are and has made provision to clothe us with His redemptive love. Like Jason, each of us must come to terms with the fact that if God is going to clothe us, we must address our willingness or lack of it to let Him undress our rage. This coming to terms leads us to the next stage of bringing our losses to resolution—facing the full impact of rage's rule. I'll meet you in the next chapter.

▼

CHAPTER 10

Conviction: Facing the Full Impact of Rage's Rule

RAGE IN ITS MANY FACES can be difficult to detect. We recognize it quickly when it is overtly explosive and abusive, but it takes more discernment to spot it when it is covert and passive.

One of the best scriptural examples of rage in its most familiar expression—the flame-throwing kind—can be seen in Daniel 3. Remember the three men who were thrown into a furnace for not bowing down to the king's idol? The story begins when Daniel's three companions refuse to be manipulated into compromising their relationship with God by worshiping an idol fabricated by King Nebuchadnezzar, the most powerful person on earth at the time. Without a doubt, he was used to getting his way in all matters.

The men who worked for him were appropriately diabolical in maintaining their king's evil and ultimate rule. Listen to their plan for ridding their land of "vermin

Jews" and bringing down the men the king had vested
with authority in Babylon:

> At this time some astrologers came forward and
> denounced the Jews. They said to King Nebuchad-
> nezzar, " . . . You have issued a decree, O king,
> that everyone who hears the sound of the horn,
> flute, zither, lyre, harp, pipes and all kinds of
> music must fall down and worship the image of
> gold, and that whoever does not fall down and
> worship will be thrown into a blazing furnace.
> But there are some Jews whom you have set over
> the affairs of the province of Babylon—Shadrach,
> Meshach and Abednego—who pay no attention
> to you, O king. They neither serve your gods
> nor worship the image of gold you have set up."
> (Daniel 3:8-12)

Notice how evil in this context presents itself as a protector. The language of that protection sounds something
like this: "When you hear music of any kind, all you have
to do is fall down and worship the idol. Do this and it will
go well with you . . . certainly we wouldn't want anything
bad to happen to you. Of course, if you refuse there will
be an unfortunate consequence—you'll be thrown into the
furnace. But don't worry. You can avoid it for sure. Just
do as you're told."

The truth is, no real protection exists in evil. The
minute we begin to serve evil and believe in its protective
promise, we become vulnerable to rage's control. Listen
to the promise of Nebuchadnezzar's men: "You're safe.
You don't have to worry. You won't be thrown into the
furnace." Now look for the small print: "As long as you do
what we tell you to—bow down and worship the image."

What kind of protection is that? The decree was fabricated out of a prejudicial desire to destroy the Jews.
The politicians knew the Jews would have difficulty with

such a law and that many would resist. Their plan was to destroy the people they hated while looking like good guys who'd given them a perfectly simple choice. In reality, they couldn't wait to spot a Jew breaking this new law so they could execute punishment. Listen to a paraphrase of the previous chapter, observing how the king's men play their cards with the king:

> Oh, by the way, King, we thought you should know that all is not well. The people are doing well, that's not the problem. You would be proud of the loyalty with which they serve you. You're truly a hero. But there are some Jews whom you have set over the affairs of the province of Babylon. We think their names are Shadrach, Meshach, and Abednego. These fellows aren't paying any attention to you. In fact, they don't serve your gods or worship your golden image. When the music starts to play, they go on about their business as though they hear nothing. You know what the law says, King. You must not let the people see that there is insurrection from within the palace, especially Jewish insurrection. No, that would never do. You'd lose everyone's respect. People will start to walk all over you, and you can't have that.

The king's men knew exactly what kind of response such news would elicit from their power-hungry king:

> Furious with rage, Nebuchadnezzar summoned Shadrach, Meshach and Abednego. So these men were brought before the king, and Nebuchadnezzar said to them, "Is it true . . . that you do not serve my gods or worship the image of gold that I have set up? Now . . . if you are ready to fall down and worship the image I made, very good. But if you do

not worship it, you will be thrown immediately into a blazing furnace. Then what god will be able to rescue you from my hand?" (3:13-15)

We don't have a full picture of how the king looked or spoke in his fury, but I get the feeling that he disguised his rage in soothing tones that held out false promises. Again, rage can appear as a benevolent protector—as long as it gets its way.

I picture the king sitting on his throne with a forced smile on his face, in control, staring directly into the eyes of each man as though looking for fear to rise up and drive him to his knees at any moment. He fully expected the three men to yield and beg his forgiveness.

The red-eyed, fire-breathing kind of rage is often masked and does not play the trump card (explosive fury) unless called to do so. Rage rises to the occasion but does not rise any higher than it must to maintain control. No doubt you have been in the presence of many rageful people who were completely calm, reserved, and under control. What did you feel emanating from that cool exterior? Did you sense the heat of the furnace that threatened to consume you if you did not comply then and there? When it goes unchallenged, rage is a friendly fire. Disobey its rule and it becomes a furnace of fury.

Having given the three men another chance to save themselves, the king sat back in his chair and waited for the apology and the worship. Look at what he got:

> Shadrach, Meshach and Abednego replied to the
> king, "O Nebuchadnezzar, we do not need to defend
> ourselves before you in this matter. If we are thrown
> into the blazing furnace, the God we serve is able
> to save us from it, and he will rescue us from your
> hand, O king. But even if he does not, we want you
> to know, O king, that we will not serve your gods

or worship the image of gold you have set up."
(3:16-18)

I wish we could see this on video. I can't help but
laugh as I hear the opening line: "O Nebuchadnezzar."
When the king hears his subjects so easily addressing
him on a first-name basis, I can see that calm exterior
beginning to crack as the veins in his neck enlarge and
his brow begins to sweat. With each word of truth, his
eyes get smaller until they shoot death in every direction.
His hands begin to tremble with fury until he can hardly
restrain himself. By the last line, "we will not serve your
gods or worship the image of gold you have set up," the
king is shouting orders in all directions: "Turn up the
furnace seven times and throw them in!"

There it is—rage in all its glory. It threw its trump
card and began to sweep the table in triumph.

But just as the king began to mouth the words "that
will teach them and anyone else who wishes to defy me,"
he looked up and saw none other than a fourth man in the
furnace who looked "like a son of the gods." In astonish-
ment, rage looked up to see the sweeping hand of God's
host reclaiming His faithful servants. Nebuchadnezzar
was left to see with his own eyes a God who saves men
from the fire of a king's hottest fury.

DEVELOPING CONVICTION

The moment we begin to follow truth, our hearts become
strengthened for a battle between rage-driven avoidance and truthful confrontation and resolution. Shadrach,
Meshach, and Abednego were men of conviction who
believed death in the arms of truth was better than
life in the arms of rage. Had they fallen down to worship, they would have allowed rage to charade as peace.
Their refusal to worship left them free to love God and be
loved by Him. God's love transcended Nebuchadnezzar's

blaze and loosed the men to walk freely with Him through the fire.

In our indebtedness to kings other than Jesus, we buy into rage's avoidance plan time and again. Each time we do, we become more indentured to evil and less able to overcome it. Evil is selfish and jealous, unable to share glory with anyone. The text reveals this to be true—everyone had to worship the king's idol or die. Evil will destroy any sense of personal value we have. That's why women or men who live in abusive environments are, with the passage of time, less able to leave. Self is destroyed, leaving a lifeless, mechanical shell in its place.

Rage's false protection plan pits one loss against another and then forces us to choose the lesser of two losses. It paints a vivid picture of the worst case scenario and plays our fear against any hope that would suggest this scenario might not be as bad as we think. Going back to the story in Daniel 3, we can see how rage employed the tactic I just described.

What was the worst case scenario? A horrific death in a blazing furnace. Death is scary enough. Death by torture is even worse. Maybe the three Jewish men had heard stories about the king's furnace. They could certainly visualize the ordeal and conclude they would try to avoid it at all costs.

With a gruesome picture in place, rage could then present something that, by comparison, was a piece of cake. "What's more valuable—your lives or your religious beliefs?" The insidious nature of rage's game is that if we try to protect one value by betraying another, we lose both. The only answer is to opt out of the game entirely—to refuse to play. That's what happened in Daniel 3.

I believe there is a supernatural dynamic to this game and that Satan is involved in the effort to convince us that it's the only game in town. I believe we must understand the real role he plays if we are going to blow rage's whole cover.

HOW SATAN DRAWS US INTO A DEADLY GAME

To blame everything on Satan is to avoid responsibility
for our own part in making choices that lead to the mechanisms we use for avoiding loss. To blame everything on
ourselves is to misunderstand the real role Satan plays
as the magistrate of evil. The truth lies somewhere in
between the two extremes. The moment we begin to avoid
resolving loss, we open the door for Satan to manipulate
and dictate with deceptive and divisive tools of destruction. Perhaps the best way to illustrate this is to discuss
the progression away from resolution.

Unresolved Loss Baits the Trap

Ted came to the group weekly with the same story: He
wanted to get his compulsive overeating under control.
Each week he returned feeling defeated, frustrated, hopeless, and out of control. He left each group meeting feeling strong, but within a few days he'd completely forget
anything helpful he or anyone else had said. After each
defeating week he said, "I feel like I'm back at square one.
I'm tired of starting over."

Without minimizing the complexity of a disorder such
as Ted's, I want to highlight his avoidance pattern. Until
Ted could understand why he chose food over reality, he
could not resist his urge to eat. He was caught in a vicious
cycle that kept him from discovering his real pain.

Within two weeks of beginning the group, Ted told
everyone that he grew up in a dysfunctional family. His
father was extremely overbearing, and his mother was
the victim of repeated verbal, as well as physical, abuse.
Ted witnessed much of the abuse and was repeatedly told
by his father that women were worthless pieces of trash.
When Ted tried to side with or protect his mother, his
father became enraged and took it out on her. He would
force Ted to watch the beating and would finish by telling
him it was his fault for taking her side.

Ted reported his experiences with almost no feeling. He had always remembered the beatings and seemed surprised by everyone's strong reaction to the injustice and terror of what he described. He told the story the way many abuse victims do, as a narrator or third party rather than someone who suffered.

Needless to say, I suspected that Ted carried immense guilt and a deep conviction that told him, "When bad things happen, it's your fault. Not only that, but if you try to help someone in pain, you will make their pain worse."

Ted could not immediately see any connection between his eating and the stories he told. He had a difficult time letting anyone in the group feel for him. When someone did, he became quiet, almost frozen. Given his father's reaction and treatment of his mother when he let his feelings show, it was easy to understand why he was so frozen and unable to feel. His feelings were dangerous. They were responsible for hurting people.

Ted's eating was his way of managing and hiding his feelings. Whenever something happened that began to arouse emotion, he immediately turned to food. Not only was he afraid of his feelings, but of everyone else's as well. He therefore had a difficult time in relationships with other people. His weight made him unappealing to women and unable to participate in many activities. It was a safety that protected him from others and others from him. It was the only defense he really had.

Each week, Ted came to the group and talked in circles. Talking was all he knew how to do. Like eating, it was his mechanism for controlling and suppressing his feelings. The only time he was silent was when someone began to relate to and feel for his story. He didn't feel anything then either. It was as though his body was present, but the rest of him went somewhere else.

Ted needed a lot of time to "defrost." He also needed a safe place to watch people feel strongly without having those strong feelings cause something bad to happen.

What am I avoiding?

He needed to have his avoidance patterns exposed so he could see why he was so trapped. Over time, Ted's pattern became obvious. It presented itself in various stages.

Making promises: In the first stage, Ted made promises. Each week he listened to input from the group and graciously received it, saying, "I'll do that," or "I'll spend some time this week thinking about that." His promises did not come from any real sense of commitment to the truth. Rather, they were his way of making sure that no one got angry with him. He couldn't refuse or object because it takes emotion to do that. He had to give in to whatever someone said. I believe if someone had told him to jump off a building, he would have responded with the same enthusiastic, appreciative tone, "I'll have to try that."

Eliminating healthy choices: Each week the group encouraged Ted to exercise some options that would lead to at least some success with his food addiction. Other strugglers in the group repeatedly gave Ted their phone numbers, encouraging him to call when he wanted to eat. Again, he would promise to call, but during the week when he was tempted to binge, he immediately eliminated each choice with rationalizations:

▼ "It's too late to call, I don't want to wake anyone up."

▼ "I've already eaten a little bit, I might as well go ahead and blow it. It won't help to talk to anyone anyway."

▼ "I'm not that critical. I can handle it. I'll just go do something else."

Lying to himself: Having eliminated healthy options, he argued with himself about what he would do. He would tell himself he wasn't going to eat. Listen to the subtle self-deception in one of his inner monologues:

"I think I'll go for a walk. I don't want to sit around

the house, I feel too bored. Where will I walk? I think I'll go by the park. I know there's a hot dog stand there, but I won't take any money so I can't buy one. Well, maybe I'll take a little bit. I might need to stop by the store on the way home to get some cat food."

At the park, "I'll walk on this side by the playground. There aren't any food places here, and the hot dog stand is all the way on the other side. Wow, look at that kid with that ice cream cone. That sure looks good. I can't eat that. I can't control myself with ice cream. Gee, I can't stand around here and watch him eat that. I guess I'll go to the other side of the park. I'll just swing by the hot dog stand. Maybe I'll see someone there I know. I would like to talk to someone today."

At the hot dog stand, "Boy, they sure smell good. I'll just go talk to the girl selling hot dogs. I bet she's busy today. I won't buy one, I'll just look. I can go back to my group this week and tell them how good I was. They'll be amazed at my ability to go to my favorite hot dog stand and not eat one hot dog. I'm thirsty. I'll buy a Pepsi. That's it. Just a small one."

Moments later to the girl selling hot dogs, "I'll have three hot dogs and a large Diet Pepsi, please."

Later, after the hot dogs, "I think I'll go home. Oh well, I knew I was going to blow it. I'm just too weak. Those guys expect too much from me anyway."

Selective memory: Some aspects of Ted's memory were remarkable. He could retell a story in such graphic detail; it was like being there. Each week his reporting to the group was specific and detailed, but when we tried to get him to focus on himself, he spoke vaguely. Things just happened; he didn't know how. He couldn't remember why he wanted to eat or what was happening around him when he began to feel the need to eat.

Once he reported that he'd had a long conversation with his mother over the weekend. He remarked that this was unusual since their conversations were typically brief. When we asked him to share what they had talked about he said, "Oh, just general things. I can't really remember. We talked about my job, her garden—you know, nothing important."

It took a great deal of work and effort to help Ted remember the conversation, but by the end of the group, he was saying, in the same narrative style, that his mother told him how unhappy she was and that she was thinking about leaving his father. She went on to tell him everything his father had done to her since the last time they talked, and urged Ted to keep their conversation a secret.

The group was quick to ask Ted if he'd gone on an eating binge after that conversation. He paused, looking puzzled, and admitted that he had. Ted still couldn't connect with his feelings, but that group was a turning point. He saw a relationship between his conversation with his mother and food. He also noticed how he conveniently forgot all about the most important part of the phone call. He realized he forgets a lot of important things. He began to wonder why.

Ted was not consciously aware of his avoidance mechanisms. He didn't understand why he did the things he did. He had lots of labels for his behavior. He had many names for himself. He had plenty of guilt and frustration over having repeatedly tried to battle overeating with no success. What he didn't realize was that food and talking were two of the rage walls that kept his healthy emotion and historical losses out of his present world. They helped him manage his feelings and maintain his relational safety, thus giving him a sense of control.

Where does Ted leave off and Satan begin? Does Ted need prayer and deliverance, or confrontation and discipline? The answer is both. Satan's role with Ted was to keep him living in a world of illusion, insulated from reality. How did Satan accomplish this? That's not as easy to answer, but he seems to deceive his victims that:

▼ Reality is too frightening to look at.

▼ Facing it will be so overwhelming that either insanity or death will follow.

▼ When reality comes, everything we were afraid it would be will be true and then everyone will know who we really are.

▼ Looking at it isn't going to change things anyway.

Satan's tactic involves threatening us with fear and hopelessness. It creates an irrational terror that seems completely real to us. The lies he gets us to believe become strongholds in which we hide.

What we say to our own Nebuchadnezzars depends largely on our willingness to see the cold truth about rage and to denounce its protective charade. Once we've begun to tenaciously hold on to the truth we have gained, regardless of the threats rage throws at us, we begin to see the real damage that our refusal to resolve loss with God's help has done, not only to ourselves but also to our relationship with Him and others. The stage is then set for repentance—the journey out of rage's rule into God's Kingdom.

▼

CHAPTER 11

Repentance: Inviting God to Rescue Us

THE LONG-TERM EFFECT of unresolved loss is twofold: it distorts our view of ourselves and others, and it distorts our view of God. When rage becomes the corrective lens we wear to see the world and ourselves, we become blind to loss. We are therefore doomed to continually repeat the same losses and to reinforce the pattern of distortion until we cannot see our own or others' authenticity. Rage worn over time prejudices our spiritual and intuitive eyes to mistrust, and makes us suspicious of all representatives of the truth.

We see this fact in the gospels as Jesus battles with the Pharisees to get them to open their eyes to the truth about Him. In Mark 4, Jesus tells His disciples:

"The secret of the kingdom of God has been given to you. But to those on the outside everything is said in parables so that, 'they may be ever seeing but

173

never perceiving, and ever hearing but never understanding; otherwise they might turn [from their
rage] and be forgiven!'" (verses 10-12)

In our lives, as in the disciples', the judgment and
opinions of others have had greater impact on our thinking and behavior than the judgment and opinions of God.
Jesus' statement on this matter was profound and must
not be interpreted as condemning or sectarian. Restated,
it might read something like this:

> Those who hold to their own distorted judgments
> and opinions about themselves, others, and God will
> remain outside the Kingdom of God. The secret of
> the Kingdom is mercy. They will refuse to under-
> stand it because all of their concepts are devel-
> oped around a rage-distorted picture of the world.
> They can't allow themselves to see new things that
> could threaten to shed light on the fragility of their
> present state. They can't really hear the truth
> because it would require rampant restructuring and
> reordering of their lives. In their view, there is no
> second chance if a first attempt at growth fails. No
> change is safer than the risk of destruction. Their
> prejudices form protective walls around them and
> keep them safe in their familiar condemnation but
> restrict them from ever experiencing God's mercy
> and love.

DISTORTED VIEWS OF GOD

Not only does rage block out or reshape past loss and
blind us to the cycle of loss and unfulfillment we create
in our current relationships, but it also intercepts and
scrambles God's message to us about Himself. Questions
regarding God's motives, His willingness, and His interest in us are raised when we see Him as an adversary

rather than a loving Father.

Failure to bring legitimate resolution to loss results in at least two distorted views of God:

▼ We fail to see that God's purpose is to restore the relationship between Him and ourselves.
▼ We fail to understand that God's love for us is unconditional and irrevocable.

When our efforts to resolve conflict in relationships fail, rather than turning our focus to Christ, we try even harder to rely more on ourselves to get our needs met. This inevitably results in placing even more pressure on others to come through for us. Our propensity toward doing this is rooted in our distorted views of God and His character. Legitimate resolution of loss helps us develop an ear for the heartbeat of God. As we learn to rest our heads on His breast, we are restored to a clearer perception. The rage-shield of avoidance is penetrated by the truth that:

▼ God restored us because He loved us.
▼ God loved us when we were in sin. Turning away from sin by turning to Him with our unmet needs will be met with the joy of a waiting Father.
▼ The discovery of our "hidden agendas" is no surprise to God.

His heart never skipped a beat when we saw the truth about ourselves. On the contrary, the reason we couldn't hear it beating before was because we couldn't see our need to rest our heads on His breast; we chose instead to lend our ears to lesser gods of comfort.

Our response toward these truths is the beginning of repentance from our devotion to rage as our protector rather than God. Repentance is not a decision as much as it is the result of one. In turning away from our avoidance and posturing our ears toward the truth, we begin to see deep resolution of loss as possible and necessary.

The Truth Still Sets Captives Free

The only way to eliminate rage is to eliminate its cause. At the root of all rage is shame, a byproduct of unresolved loss. Without experiencing a restoration of our value to a God who paid the penalty for our sins, loss will always be an unacceptable prospect that we will resist with all of the rage we can muster.

Rage, as resistance to loss, is much like a degenerative disease. The longer we have it, the more disabled we become. Over time, it affects literally every part of us. Loss of conscious contact with reality and truth is an effect of rage. The Bible refers to it as "hard-heartedness" or, in its most extreme and perhaps irreversible sense, "reprobate," which describes someone who has reached such depravity of spirit that he has no capacity to feel the impact of truth.

The greatest difficulty in helping people eradicate rage is to get them to stop trying to eradicate it themselves. With so much effort aimed at getting rid of rage, it actually becomes the object of a person's attention, fascination, and energy. I believe there is a diabolically narcissistic aspect to rage. In other words, it feeds on our attention. As long as we focus on eradicating rage rather than accepting and resolving loss, we will never escape rage's rule.

Experiencing, feeling, and resolving loss necessitates a search for meaning. Since no real meaning in life exists apart from God, we are eventually bound to find that His love has the capacity to receive us in our despair and breathe hope into those parts of us that are weary from the search. Such discovery is the beginning of deliverance. Once our rage-controlled parts have felt love's first blow and our weary souls find comfort, rage's power to seduce us is significantly reduced.

I'm so afraid to trust the Lord to meet my needs.

TRANSFORMED BY GOD

I have witnessed this discovery with courageous men and women who have not only begun a search for meaning, but have been remarkably transformed by God's powerful and restorative love. One of the first and most significant examples of transforming discovery that I witnessed occurred in a men's group one night a few years ago.

Joe had been a member of the group from its inception. He was dedicated to resolving loss in his life, and he had a great deal to resolve. He never knew his father and was abandoned on a doorstep by his mother before he was three years old. Fortunately, he was taken in by a family who finished raising him in a relatively stable environment.

Joe had been working for several months to reach a point of trust with God before he could allow himself to feel the full impact of being left by his mother. For him, the feeling was as close to death as he could imagine. He didn't know how long he was on the doorstep, but had a faint memory of being cold. Joe wept a lot over the months as he dealt with his abandonment. The fact that he was alive seemed difficult to accept since a young, but big, part of him felt he had been unwanted and discarded. His theology could grasp the truth that God wanted him, but his heart had been deeply wounded, making it difficult to imagine or understand how that could be true.

One night, Joe came to the group greatly agitated. We had been talking about rage for several weeks, and Joe knew he had a pattern of destructive and violent fantasies for as long as he could remember. As an adolescent, he painted his bedroom walls black and would lie in the crack between his bed and wall until he went to sleep. On this particular evening, Joe explained that he wanted to explode violently. He saw himself unleashing a rage that was both terrifying and attractive. Over the months, Joe had shared a great deal with the group. We saw his confession as an opportunity to usher him into the arms of Jesus—rage and all.

I asked Joe to picture himself standing in front of Jesus with all of his rage. This was difficult for him to do because of how violent he felt. He was afraid to imagine what he would do or say to Jesus. I encouraged him to take the risk. I assured him that Jesus was big enough to face his rage. His experience with Jesus over the past several months had given Joe some capacity to believe that what I said might be true. What followed astounded us all.

Joe said he saw himself, full of rage, standing across from Jesus. I told him to look at Jesus and tell us what Jesus was doing. The expression on his face turned dark and almost sullen. I asked him what was happening. He said, "Jesus turned his back." My immediate thought was that Jesus wouldn't do that.

Joe began to cry. I thought it was because he felt Jesus was rejecting him. I asked him why he was crying. By this time there were sobs. With eyes closed, he said, "Jesus wants me to give it to Him. He's turned His back because He wants me to see the scars that bore the rage of others before me." The group was stunned. In a few moments Joe went from murderous rage to grateful weeping.

That evening for Joe was a turning point in his relationship with God and his reliance on rage. It didn't magically erase his pain nor did he walk out of the group problem-free. But he did leave with the knowledge that God's love and mercy had penetrated a part of him that had never been touched by anyone. Rage was a fallen giant.

Joe continues to work toward resolution of loss. Over the past two years since that evening, I have watched him grow and progress in his relationships with God and others. Sometimes his struggles are profound and the old faces of rage seem attractive. At times, God seems distant and Joe's sense of purpose seems muddled by his questions about life's hardships. But when I called to ask his permission to share this story, he told me that just thinking about it brought tears to his eyes. He wanted others to know that Jesus was big enough to love them in their rage just as he had been loved in his.

What made it possible for Joe to relinquish his rage? He had to see something bigger and more substantial than himself since he had made resolution after resolution to no avail. Upon seeing Jesus, he witnessed the unalterable truth of Isaiah 53:4 (NKJV): "He [Jesus] has borne our griefs and carried our sorrows." When Joe gave his rage to Christ he discovered that Jesus, upon receiving it, would turn around and give him what his rage had tried and failed to accomplish all along—security, love, comfort, and protection.

I really don't believe this and I'm not sure how to change my beliefs

CHAPTER 12

▼

Resolution: Incorporating Loss and Transcending Death

"TELL ME HOW to resolve loss without feeling it and I'm ready." I hear statements like that in one form or another almost every day. We are all afraid to feel pain. Perhaps it's because we have seen too many people get stuck in their pain and seemingly never get out. Maybe we don't think others will be tolerant of the time it will take to recover. Still others of us don't have enough patience with ourselves; we're still telling ourselves to snap out of it and get on with life.

Some of us are willing to hurt if we are assured of a definable beginning and end to the pain. I wish it were that easy. I am coming to a place in my own life where I accept the fact that I will always feel a certain degree of pain when I see dads holding their little boys, because the picture album of my life has a lot of empty pages in that area. But I'm learning that the pain is good and productive because it reminds me I still need a Daddy.

ı can't fill my album with someone else's pictures or adopt someone else's memories, but I can continue to discover God's Fathering character. That gives me somewhere to go with my pain and helps me accept the truth about my less than ideal life.

I left much of my own picture album empty because something said you should have a dad in those pictures—that's the ideal. I felt ashamed to put pictures in it that were a representation of my abandonment and brokenness. Then I discovered something important. I realized that the Bible, a photo album of sorts, was full of pictures representing the conflict, loss, and brokenness of families. Nothing about reality was edited. We human beings have a propensity to hide that of which we're ashamed.

When we determine to resolve our losses, the first pain we encounter is the exposure of our shame. A gigantic relinquishment of self-protective control occurs when we begin to fill the empty pages with our significant losses. The second pain is that of the loss itself. Resolution at this level means having access to our feelings—all of them.

Since we have learned over time to hide, stuff, and deny a large percentage of our feelings, we can and often do hit walls in the resolution process marked "Entrance Forbidden." At these junctures we need the help of God and others to begin liberating the feelings we've locked behind those vow-made buttresses of resistance.

STEPPING TOWARD PAIN

Most of us are willing to do whatever we must to get out of pain. Driven by the incentive to be pain-free, we endure a fairly significant amount of suffering as long as we believe there is a guarantee that we won't have to feel any more heartache. I call it the "Inoculation Doctrine." It is based on the idea that if we do certain painful but necessary things, we will be given spiritual immunity to suffering and loss. While it appeals to the parts of us that don't want to hurt, its message is false and unbiblical.

Even if God magically wiped out our past so that there was no loss to resolve, within a matter of days or weeks we could experience significant loss that may change our lives permanently. In order to resolve our feelings about the change, we must walk into, not away from, our loss and spend time sitting in our pain.

Sounds like fun, doesn't it? I'm sure some people wonder, "What are you, some kind of pain freak? Do you get off on 'sitting in pain'?" Actually, I have just as many exits from pain as the next person. Since most of us don't like pain, it seems logical that we would do whatever we could to avoid it. As tempted as we are to follow the pain-free route, however, we must not. Listen to what Solomon says in Ecclesiastes 7:2-4:

> It is better to go to a house of mourning
> than to go to a house of feasting,
> for death is the destiny of every man;
> the living should take this to heart.
> Sorrow is better than laughter,
> because a sad face is good for the heart.
> The heart of the wise is in the house of mourning,
> but the heart of fools is in the house of
> pleasure.

Sounds morose to our modern ears. Why should anyone want to walk into grief when given the opportunity to feel good? What could we possibly learn from death? Solomon's answer in my own loose paraphrase is: a more meaningful existence through life-preserving wisdom and power that can face loss and resolve it.

Resolution is the process of incorporating loss as something that defines ours and others' mortality while working fully within our mortal limits to embrace all of life—including death. That means that the more we

resolve, the more mortal we become and the more dependent we are in our mortality to find comfort, understanding, and strength outside ourselves.

Resolution keeps us from becoming overrighteous,
overwise, or overwicked and thereby foolish. Solomon's
words again:

> Do not be overrighteous,
>   neither be overwise—
>   why destroy yourself?
> Do not be overwicked,
>   and do not be a fool—
>   why die before your time?
> It is good to grasp the one
>   and not let go of the other.
>   The man who fears God will avoid all extremes.
>   (Ecclesiastes 7:16-18)

Risking Pain

Resolution balances us so that we may live and die with
dignity regardless of the circumstances under which we
experience both. To sit in our pain means being willing
to enter a period of time when our lives feel more empty
than full and to wrestle with the fear that perhaps life
will never be as full again.

The biblical pattern is undeniable. Pain before pleas-
ure, suffering before joy, and grief before celebration. It
has nothing to do with God's need to see us hurt, but
with His desire to restore us. After the Fall there was
no end to suffering, no relief from pain, and no answer
to grief. When we submit ourselves to the biblical pattern
of resolution, we repeatedly invite the miracle of Christ's
incarnation. If we are willing to risk the pain, we will
discover the power of God to transcend our circumstances
and fellowship with us in our moment of despair and
agony. Heaven comes to earth, and the bond between
Father and child is reestablished.

In *The Problem of Pain*, C.S. Lewis explains that the sole purpose for which we were created was to experience this bond. He paints a clear picture of what we struggle with in the process of resolving loss:

> The place for which He (God) designs them (humans) in His scheme of things is the place they are made for. When they reach it their nature is fulfilled and their happiness attained: a broken bone in the universe has been set, the anguish is over. When we want to be something other than the thing God wants us to be, we must be wanting what, in fact, will not make us happy. Those Divine demands which sound to our natural ears most like those of a despot and least like those of a lover, in fact marshall us where we should want to go if we knew what we wanted.[1]

When I read those words, I can't help but smile as I think about all the people I have watched in the critical moments of choosing to make the exodus from rage to resolution. While moving from rage's death grip to the open arms of Christ could have been a moment of ecstatic celebration—"Free at last!"—more than often it was one of agony. Rage's clutch had seemed so secure, familiar, and caring. Landing in the arms of Christ at first felt like being utterly abandoned.

Once we realize that rage has been serving as a protector to our abandoned parts, we often feel an overwhelming desire to deny the strength of its power to keep us from resolving loss. To admit that we are happier in our self-made pain of avoidance than in the unknown legitimate pain of resolution is to realize that we would rather be smothered by rage than feel the first aching pain of our spiritual emptiness.

The deepest suffering in connection with any kind of departure from our rage occurs more after the fact than during. When we answer freedom's call, the legitimate suffering begins when we cross the threshold of real life. Here we meet our mortality face to face. Without rage to help, no mechanism exists to offer us a sense of self-omnipotence nor avoidance to usher us into a world that obeys our orders. We are completely out of control—and at the mercy of God.

Out of the womb again, this time into the hands of a heavenly Father, our soul's first response to freedom's air is like that of a newborn—a gasp, a sputter, a primal cry, and finally, a wanton lust for more.

GIVING WAY TO HONOR

Legitimate resolution identifies and undresses our rage. Once naked, we are washed and prepared to receive the adornments of a Father whose express purpose is to lavish His love on us with reckless abandon. Resolution is a homecoming of sorts. God celebrates the return of His prodigal child and clothes his naked shamefulness with honor.

Why, then, do we so fiercely resist coming home to our Father's arms? The answer is our propensity to choose mere existence and survival over real and eternal spiritual life.

We have never encountered love, hope, peace, and joy as they really are. Even in our best moments and relationships, we can find only dim reflections of what God offers in His perfect character. In exchanging rich spiritual life for familiar existence, we have grown deaf and blind to the ultimate treasures in our Father's house. This is what Jesus was talking about when He admonished people to evaluate their deepest values.

> "Do not store up for yourselves treasures on earth, where moth and rust destroy, and where thieves break in and steal. But store up for yourselves treasures in heaven, where moth and rust do not

destroy, and where thieves do not break in and
steal. For where your treasure is, there your heart
will be also." (Matthew 6:19)

When we pour our lives into existing, surviving, and
taking the path of least resistance in an attempt to protect ourselves and what little we value, we are doomed to
having moths and rust eat away at the fiber of our souls.
We surround ourselves with trinkets and trophies hoping
to hear them say, "Your existence has been meaningful."
Israel was guilty of this when Jeremiah recorded God's
prophetic word to His people:

"What fault did your fathers find in me,
   that they strayed so far from me?
They followed worthless idols
   and became worthless themselves.
They did not ask, 'Where is the LORD . . . ?'
my people have exchanged their Glory
   for worthless idols. . . .
They have forsaken me,
   the spring of living water,
and have dug their own cisterns,
   broken cisterns that cannot hold water."
         (Jeremiah 2:5-6,11,13)

Existence is bargaining with people and circumstances
in order to maintain our self-made survival shelters. By
stark contrast, life is conquering circumstances to maintain inseparable relationship with the Lord who is our
treasure and glory. He fills our lives with purpose and
meaning as we actively pursue a daily pilgrimage aimed
at arriving at death's door with a passport to eternal life
securely in hand.

Oswald Chambers clearly defined this spiritual journey through life when he wrote in *Still Higher for His
Highest*:

The thought of pilgrimage sank deep into the Hebrew mind, and the note of the sojourner is essentially the note of the Christian. Instead of being pilgrims and strangers on the earth, we become citizens of this order of things and entrench ourselves there, and the statements of Jesus have no meaning. The genius of the Spirit of God is to make us Pilgrims. . . . The life of faith does not consist of acts of worship or of great self-denial and heroic virtues [trinkets and trophies], but of all the daily conscious acts of our lives.[2]

Life is pilgrimage—an active pursuit of truth. Existence is hiding in the trenches of avoidance, allowing the world's godless order to dominate and direct our fate. In Romans 8:35-39, we see the remarkable difference between Christian pilgrimage and ignoble pursuits:

Who shall separate us from the love of Christ? Shall trouble or hardship or persecution or famine or nakedness or danger or sword? As it is written: "For your sake we face death all day long; we are considered as sheep to be slaughtered." No, in all these things we are more than conquerors through him who loved us. For I am convinced that neither death nor life, neither angels nor demons, neither the present nor the future, nor any powers, neither height nor depth, nor anything else in all creation, will be able to separate us from the love of God that is in Christ Jesus our Lord.

Crisis and loss are addressed within the context of inseparable relationship with Christ. The greater the conflict or loss, the more powerful His love to sustain us through it. The question, "Who shall separate us from the love of Christ?" is not rooted in fatalistic doom. It's not focused on the terrible hand life deals. It is not passively waiting for evil to respond by striking the fatal blow of death. Rather, it challenges us to fix our eyes on the greatness of God's love.

THE POWER OF THE LIVING GOD

Too often, we are chased into the trenches of avoidance by the intimidating sound of enemy troops all around. But it's not the greatness of the Enemy's army that sends us running; it's the lack of experience of having Someone greater at our side. The power of evil enlarges one-hundred fold when we have a powerless love with which to thwart it. God's rebuke to Israel's fathers for forsaking Him was directed at their abandonment of responsibility to teach their children of the God whose powerful love rescued them from Egypt and brought them into a land of promise and prosperity (Jeremiah 2:5-9).

Many generations later, we are the children of fathers who failed to teach us about the power of the Living God, One whose love cannot be diminished by the works of evil or the circumstances of life. We have learned to accept wimpish love and fully expect God to be waiting in the avoidance trench with us as though He's as much at a loss for a solution as we are.

Wimpish love cannot affirm, protect, accept, forgive, provide, heal, or give dignity and honor to any of us. When we have been disillusioned by the impotence and emptiness of what we believe to be real love, we turn to idols—our own defensive control expressed in a few or countless "isms." We sacrifice ourselves to their daily demands and then wait for them to fill and satisfy our needs. We are deaf to the loving call of our Father, beckoning us to come home for the banquet.

In the morass of daily living, we forget to reflect on who we are. God's purpose in teaching us to endure life's hardships, past and present, and to resolve loss is to distill and clarify our value as His children so we might see ourselves and others as His treasures and recognize the absolute, incomprehensible power of His love. Honor is the product of such recognition. It is a permanent deposit of value, given on our behalf and paid to our account with unretractable love, grace, and mercy.

Once we decide to resolve our losses legitimately by sitting with God in our pain, we must turn our faces toward the wilderness of grief, where we meet our pain and God's grace—a union that begins the process of integrating the parts of us that have been torn and shredded by life's losses.

▼

CHAPTER 13

Integration: Crossing from Grief to Grace

MARK SAT SILENTLY across from me, hands in his lap, eyes staring at the carpet on my office floor. I waited for him to emerge from his internal dialogue. We'd been talking for quite some time, and the morning had been a productive one. Mark was beginning to recognize his mechanisms for avoiding loss in his life.

He had a lot of unresolved loss and for the past several months spent each week in my office struggling to reconcile the past he'd just as soon forget with the present he was trying to direct and maintain. This was the week he would later call his "breakthrough" as well as his "point of no return."

Once he saw his avoidance patterns with his own eyes, Mark knew things would never be the same. Almost before realizing it, he found one foot in the wilderness of grief. What would the rest of him do? Would he give in to the voices of resistance that said, "You can't go there—it's

unknown. You think life is hard now, just wait . . ."?
Would he bargain with God: "Isn't there another way to do
this? Do I have to go?" Would he vacillate between his new
insight and old beliefs? There were so many choices; none
of them were very appealing to the avoidance-addicted
parts of him. He looked at me and asked (as though his
being there was my doing), "Now what?"

NOW WHAT?

Now what are the most difficult small words I know. It
doesn't matter how many times I hear them; when someone arrives at the borderland of his or her own rage and
the Kingdom of God's grace, the words remain difficult.

Perhaps you're asking the same question. You've
read a book about loss, avoidance, rage, and the need to
grieve. You've been given a clear picture of the problem.
You've identified several losses in your own life and hope-
fully realized that you're having difficulty legitimately
resolving those losses. Maybe a hornet's nest of questions
have been stirred up—questions you thought you'd put
to rest.

On my next meeting with Mark, I asked him how his
week had gone. He looked at me and shook his head. "I
had a rough week. Our last talk stirred up a lot of old
garbage. I don't like the fact that it's still there. I thought
I'd gotten rid of all that stuff." I nodded as he talked. What
felt bad to him was a clear signal to me that his inner need
to grieve his losses was gaining momentum. Our talk was
just another purposeful maneuver on God's part to help
Mark see his many walls of resistance. I controlled my
thrill over what I recognized as a new beginning; Mark
would not have been able to appreciate my excitement.
As far as he was concerned, the world was coming to an
end, and he didn't like it one bit.

Satan tries to keep us believing that we are better
off clinging to our resistance to resolve loss than we are

193

INTEGRATION: CROSSING FROM GRIEF TO GRACE

embracing the parts of ourselves and our lives that seem weak, insignificant, shameful, or downright intolerable. Remember Truddi Chase's belief about integration? She was convinced that true comfort could come only from a rage (avoidance) she would always hold. She never entered the Kingdom of God's grace where she could become more whole, because she was unwilling to journey through the frightening wilderness of grief.

The "now what?" question is difficult because I find it impossible to tell people, "this is it," without feeling their panic and disbelief firing a forceful glare in my direction. "You brought me out into the middle of nowhere only to tell me that we're here?" How do I explain? What can I say that will bring about a greater sense of "things are going to be fine"? The answer—nothing. People must experience the feelings of shock and anger—the sense of being lost and alone. It's part of the wilderness experience.

At this point, I say, "We're really not in the middle of nowhere. This is the wilderness. At some point, we must all visit this place. It just seems like the middle of nowhere because you can't see anything familiar, tame, or safe by your standards." This "comfort" isn't always well-received, as you can imagine.

HOW LONG?

The next question is "How long do I have to be here?" I'm no better at answering this question than "now what?" We journey in and out of the wilderness of grief throughout our lives. For people beginning to resolve old losses, the stay may be lengthy. I usually prepare people by saying, "I can't tell you how long you have to be here, but you should plan to get to know this place." Again, this response doesn't go over very well. Interestingly, most of the people who arrive at this point don't run when I tell them the truth. Sure, it isn't what they want to hear, but they are tired of hearing lies and false promises.

Once we begin to turn to the truth about our losses and confront our avoidance, we head toward the point of no return. But the Kingdom of God's grace isn't as far off as it seems. Between the land of rage and the wilderness of grief is a river full of His grace—Christ's blood in a Red Sea of sorts. Like in the story in Exodus, our journey from the land of rage begins when we say yes to Jesus' call to trust and follow Him.

With the Holy Spirit acting as our Moses, we are compelled to follow Him to an unknown and mysterious place. When we reach the Red Sea and turn to see our enemies in hot pursuit, we panic and feel sure that death is upon us. But, as in the story that mesmerized us as children, the sea opens and we cross on dry ground. As rage's soldiers enter to cross, they are consumed and buried in a sea of blood that does not permit God's children to be carried back into a world of slavery and fear.

The Old Testament images of deliverance are so powerful to me. Ageless and untarnishably relevant, they provide a backdrop from which to stage our own exodus into freedom.

THE TENSION OF INTEGRATION

Mark knew he'd come too far to go back. He was afraid of what lay ahead. He didn't like the idea of grieving. He didn't like the prospect of camping out in a place with none of the familiar comforts of his former rage-home. He felt the first pains of tension associated with integration.

To picture that tension, think about what it's like to watch a television screen that oscillates between two pictures. The lack of resolution on the screen would bother most of us. Almost immediately we'd get up, go to the "control" knob and "fix it." What works with televisions, however, does not work for the person needing to integrate. No control knob exists to fix the picture.

Part of resolving loss so we experience integration is

the willingness to feel the tension of our own oscillat-
ing screens. Sometimes the picture looks scrambled so
that nothing is clear. Other times, it rolls very slowly; we
see two pictures moving from top to bottom. Still other
times, it seems that the picture is finally clear and things
are back in focus. Looking back, looking forward, looking
in and out, over and under, back and forth—this is the
cadence of resolution.

IT'S WORTH IT

While resolution is slow, it is also sure. Over time, we feel
the effects of integration:

▼ The ability to stay with one picture for longer
periods of time without needing to find a control
knob or change channels.
▼ A greater sense of stability in our relationships.
▼ The ability to access our thoughts and feelings
in a way that allows tension but does not end in a
blur of confusion that leaves us without direction or
choices.
▼ The absence of guilt that pulls us in ten directions at one time.
▼ The ability to trust our own choices and allow
failure as a part of the learning process associated
with being human.
▼ A deeper sense of being loved and a greater ability to love others.

Do these effects seem far away from your reality? Do
you feel as though you're never going to get there? I understand if you do, but I also am hopeful for you. Tolerate
your questions. Feel your inner tension. Reach out for
help. Talk to others who are grieving. Share your losses
even if they seem insignificant in comparison to those
you hear others address. Risk shaking your fist at God

and asking Him, "Why?" Be willing to hear His answer: "Follow Me into the wilderness and I will show you things about yourself, life, and your loss that you cannot see on rage's soil."

It's interesting and, at first, terrifying that the portal to the Kingdom of His grace leads to what appears to be a barren, God-forsaken land. But appearances are often misleading. The journey through the wilderness teaches us the crucial lessons we can learn no other way. We learn we must:

▼ die to our own avoidance;
▼ permit the truth to cut out the cancer of our own bitterness;
▼ relinquish our conscious defense and control mechanisms that keep us hidden and "safe";
▼ renounce our performance and control vows that keep us compartmentalized and insulated from realities that mirror losses we would rather avoid;
▼ declare the Kingdom of God and its goodness to our enslaved and weary parts.

The journey takes time. God has time. Remember these two truths—we needn't work at integration, and we only need to be willing to resolve our losses. Integration is the result of that process.

PROMISES FROM THE SHEPHERD

In Luke 15:4-7, Jesus describes His fervent love for us in a way that reveals His inexhaustible pursuit of all our lost parts that we've abandoned in fear and shame:

"Suppose one of you has a hundred sheep and loses one of them. Does he not leave the ninety-nine in the open country and go after the lost sheep until

he finds it? And when he finds it, he joyfully puts
it on his shoulders and goes home. Then he calls his
friends and neighbors together and says, 'Rejoice
with me; I have found my lost sheep.' I tell you
that in the same way there will be more rejoicing
in heaven over one sinner who repents than over
ninety-nine righteous persons who do not need to
repent."

I used to look at this passage quantitatively—Jesus
cares about all of the lost sinners "out there" and will
leave all of us "righteous people" to go find them. Because
I work with so many people who are hopelessly lost to
themselves, this passage now has a greater meaning to
me. I tell people who are dealing with unresolved loss
and sincere doubt about God's concern for their pain that
Jesus will not rest until He reaches every disconnected,
discarded, abandoned, lost part of us and reconnects those
parts with the part of us that already trusts Him.

Most Christians I encounter can trust Jesus from
some part. Mark from earlier in the chapter had no
trouble trusting Jesus with his "spiritual" needs, but
entire compartments within him had no idea that Jesus
would want to have anything to do with them. If these
aspects of him could speak, they would say they didn't
know anything about Jesus.

Our Lord intends to search out all of our lost and hidden parts and, upon finding those parts, to joyfully place
us upon His shoulders and return home in triumph over
having recovered us from our plight. Do you hear that?
He joyfully carries us! He doesn't chastise or rebuke us.

From a logical perspective, even in Jesus' time, one
lost sheep seems relatively insignificant when you have
ninety-nine in the field. But I imagine Jesus would
respond by saying, "One lost sheep is one lost sheep;
the herd isn't complete without it." This is the language
of integration.

Many of us seem quite willing to be 80-percent Christian. We don't seem to be bothered by the fact that 20 percent of our being has no concept of Christ. I hear many people say things like, "What you're saying is all well and good, but I really don't have time to get in touch with my losses. I have a busy life and too much to risk."

When we leave a few sheep to the elements and forsake the quest to find them, we never feel secure about the fate of the remaining ninety-eight or ninety-nine that are safe. People who are afraid to search for the lost parts of themselves are preoccupied with protecting what they've got. The idea of leaving the open country and searching more hostile territory for the helpless, bleating, bleeding lamb out there (or, in there, as the case may be) is terrifying. It seems a nuisance and a losing proposition.

These people are no more prepared to hear what Jesus said about a redeeming God than were the Pharisees. As long as they choose to cling to the 80 percent they will resist the process of integration and will choose rage's protection over God's every time.

In his book *A Different Drum*, M. Scott Peck remarks:

> Integrity is never painless. It requires that we
> let matters rub up against each other, that we
> fully experience the tension of conflicting needs,
> demands, and interests, that we even be emotion-
> ally torn apart by them.[1]

He goes on to suggest that integration is a painful process because it works against avoidance to reconcile conflict and resolve loss.

To integrate, we must expel our prejudices against change and invite the truth to enlarge itself within us, even if it seems too big or impossible to contain. When we eat meat, we risk choking on it. We can be sure God will remind us to slow down, chew our food, and take our time.

COURAGE AND INTEGRATION

Integration takes—and builds—courage. As we confront our own black-and-white thinking, as we allow inner tension to challengingly question the views and beliefs we hold dear, as we wrestle with the power of our human nature to avoid the truth and resist God, and as we discover how utterly helpless we are to overcome our own resistance without His help, we find we need someone to touch our lame limbs and teach us to walk upright.

Courage doesn't always feel courageous. At times, we feel our way as we move from inner compartment to inner compartment. Turning up (or on) the lights in those places is at first startling, then overwhelming. We often wish we'd never stepped into enlightenment. We look at others around us and say, "Wasn't it better to be ignorant?" Knowing eyes smile in return, and without words, we exchange determined glances that say, "I can't go back. . . . I've come too far." Remember Mark's journey? That's courage.

Integration doesn't always fare well with those we want to impress most. It's an unfortunate, but true, fact that those we look to for approval and acknowledgment during our metamorphosis will often criticize us and say in high spiritual tones, "I'm concerned about you. You're not the Christian you used to be. Things look pretty messy in your house." But during the process toward integration, things will get messy before they get clean. People who do not understand this or criticize it are acting out of fear. The more we understand a process, the less we have to fear from it.

Do people resolving loss ever resolve loss and "return to normal"? People often look at the integration process, which begins with resolving losses, as a passing stage along the same lines as adolescence or mid-life crisis. But integration is not the return to a former state, it is the arrival at a new one. Integration is not about doing or saying the right things, being with the right people, or having the latest right knowledge. It is about yielding our members to Christ one by one until all are under the blanket of His gracious love.

> Oh grief Thy hand is scarred and rough
> Oh pain the journey is enough
> to bring me to Calvary's hill.
> Oh joy Thy vision is clear and sound
> Oh courage to bleed upon the ground
> to hang with Thee on Calvary's hill.
> Oh deep resolve to conquer death
> to seize the day in final breath,
> and bring all willing to Thy place
> of life beyond Calvary's hill.
> *written by author*

Notes

Chapter 7: The Fearful Escape from Truth and Self
1. Truddi Chase, *When Rabbit Howls* (New York: E.P. Dutton, 1987), page xxvii.

Chapter 8: The Ruthless Defense Against Conflict
1. Lenore Terr, *Too Scared to Cry: Psychic Trauma in Childhood* (New York: Harper & Row, 1990), page 113.

Chapter 12: Resolution: Incorporating Loss and Transcending Death
1. C.S. Lewis, *The Problem of Pain* (New York: Macmillan, 1959), pages 40-41.
2. Oswald Chambers, *Still Higher for His Highest* (Fort Washington, PA: Christian Literature Crusade, 1970), page 119.

Chapter 13: Integration: Crossing from Grief to Grace
1. M. Scott Peck, *A Different Drum* (New York: Simon & Schuster, 1987), page 227.

Author

DAVID DAMICO is the founder and director of Christian Assisted Recovery Environments, Inc., a lay organization committed to assisting individuals struggling with unresolved losses to journey through grief in supportive, interactive, and biblically based small groups.

David's ongoing and enlarging vision is to strengthen and equip lay people in local churches to love the lost sheep within their own communities, while developing and maintaining a vision to approach the larger community of lost people with a real message of hope.

David has resided in San Diego, California, with his wife, Kellie, since 1982. They have one toy poodle, Chili, who insists on being an only child.

Afterword

THROUGHOUT THIS BOOK I have endeavored to develop a language for recognizing and dealing with rage. My insights and instruction are far from comprehensive, but perhaps you have discovered a bit more light for the loss-strewn path on which you may walk toward resolution and love. For the reflective reader who will go on to use various aspects of the book's contents to help himself and/or others, I have some important advice.

I spoke to a friend who attended a well-known Christian leader's annual seminar. During the seminar, several people approached the leader and his ministry team for help. During interviews that ranged in length from twenty minutes to an hour, he and his team asked a series of questions aimed at pinpointing the exact nature of their charge's problems. The answers led the interviewers to the conclusion that each person asking for help had been abused in childhood, in a broad range of categories, ranging from emotional abuse to Satanic ritual abuse. Most of those being interviewed were encouraged to dissect their past and find a specializing psychotherapist. While it may not have been their intent, the result of the interviewers' efforts was diagnostic pigeonholing.

To reduce someone's behavioral and relational brokenness to roots of destruction, and to treat those roots of destruction with precise, calculated, and technique-oriented bedside manner does more to dehumanize the individual than the abuse in question. As helpful as seminars, books, and other self-discovery tools may be, they are often misused in application because those of us doing the seminars, writing the books, and working to help others develop discovery tools are largely out of touch with how to heal and change ourselves. We may be able diagnose problems with pinpoint accuracy, adding to our credibility. But are we able to reach beyond our clinician's view into the genuine ministry of caring empathetically for ourselves or others?

Before you use some of this book's insights to enhance your diagnostic skills, bear in mind that such knowledge did not make it any easier for the sufferers portrayed in this book to endure the crisis of their own rage. Nor did discovering the root diagnostically result in its instantaneous extraction.

The only root killer of rage, damage, and sin I know of is love communicated over time in a safe and stable community whose purpose is to follow Christ in His most explicit directive: "This is my command: Love each other" (John 15:17).

I am grateful for whatever usefulness this book may have in painting a clearer picture of rage and its relationship to unresolved loss. I hope as you incorporate the contents of this book with your own life experience, you will discover how adequate you are to touch others in a healing way.